YOU A CHRISTIAN &MONEY

A GUIDE FOR ACHIEVING TRUE FINANCIAL FREEDOM FOR CHRISTIANS

SOLOMON CHIKAN

1

CONTENTS

1:00 INTRODUCTION..............4

2:00 WHAT IS MONEY...........12

3:00 WHY YOU A CHRISTIAN MUST AND SHOULD BE BOTHERED ABOUT MONEY..26

4:00 YOU A CHRISTIAN AND FINANCIAL SUCCESS....................................84

5:00 WHAT YOU A CHRISTIAN NEED TO BE ABLE TO ACHIEVE FINANCIAL SUCCESS....................................96

6:00 WAYS OF MAKING MONEY.....................................110

7:00 THINGS THAT YOU A CHRISTIAN MUST AND SHOULD KNOW, HAVE AND BE ABLE TO DO, TO BE ABLE TO LIVE AND MAKE MONEY IN THE WORLD..........................154

8:00 HOW YOU A CHRISTIAN SHOULD USE MONEY WHEN YOU HAVE IT.......................196

9:00 HOW YOU A CHRISTIAN SHOULD LIVE AND LOOK FOR MONEY...................................230

10:00 CASE STUDY (How to overcome the lack of money).....................................242

1:00 INTRODUCTION

This book has been written to inform and educate Christians about money.

It explains what money really is and why Christians must and should give it attention.

The book also explains what true financial success is and why you a Christian must and should seek to achieve true financial success.

I embarked on writing this book and started the YOU A CHRISTIAN AND MONEY WORKSHOP which this book serves as a manual for to inform and educate Christians about ,

(a) what money really is.

(b) how they are to live and look for it.

(c) the right attitude they should have towards it.

(d) the correct way they should use it when they get it.

In the course of my travels to various parts of the world to speak in conferences, seminars, workshops and churches, I discovered that, despite the very important role money as a resource plays in the World , Christians need it every day and must interact with it or the things acquired with it daily and the fact that the Bible talks so much about money and possessions churches are not teaching Christians about it.

I discovered amongst other things that, not only is there a high level of ignorance about money amongst Christians but most of them are ignorant of the basics of biblical finance and how they are to handle money as Christians. This has led to most of them having and living with money problems.

Prominent amongst these problems that Christians have in the area of money are,

(a) The lack of money.

Most Christians and indeed the church as a whole lacks money. Most Christians live from hand to mouth and this has affected their giving, especially to their churches and the needy.

(b)Possession of wrong attitudes towards money.

Most Christians because of their ignorance of what money really is see and relate to money wrongly.

Money has become a "god" to most of these Christians and as such they are in bondage to it. They live for it and they are ready to do anything for it. Many are even ready to kill for money.

It is my desire that with the help of the information contained in this book Christians will be educated about money so that they become well informed and equipped to know what money really is and how they can live, make it correctly, relate to it and use it correctly.

I want Christians to be able to solve the financial problems that come their way, achieve financial success and above all to be free from financial bondage.

I consider the information in this book a very important resource for Christians as they need it to be free from financial bondage. A people in bondage to money cannot be free to live life as they have been created to live by God. Freedom from financial bondage is a necessity for fruitful, impactful and abundant living. Freedom from financial bondage is therefore a must for all those who would want to live, become who God made them to be and fulfill their God ordained lives purposes on Earth.

I think all Christians should aspire to achieve this.

It is therefore with a sincere prayer that this book serves as a source of, information, knowledge and a tool for your deliverance and liberation from financial bondage that I commit it into your hands.

10

2:00 WHAT IS MONEY

When the question, WHAT IS MONEY ? is put to most people their minds go straight to the printed paper or stamped coins which are issued by the central Bank of their home country as legal tender and are used for payment for goods, services and debts.

Permit me to put the same question to you, WHAT IS MONEY TO YOU?

How do you define money? What do you see as money?

Do you also see money only as the printed paper or stamped coins issued by the Central Bank of your country which serves as legal tender in your Country and are being used for commercial transactions in your country? If you do, then I will not be surprise if you are one of those who are having and living with money problems. People who see money only as this printed paper or stamped coins are ignorant of what money really is and as such they are among people who have money problems. You will get to know why people who see money only as the printed paper or stamped coins have money problems as you read on.

The printed paper or stamped coins you use as legal tender are called money but in reality they are not what money really is.

They are merely the representation of money.

You will not see money if you go after money only with the knowledge and desire for its representative. However, if you do get it, you will not enjoy such money as it will bring you sorrows and you will not achieve and enjoy the benefits that come with doing the things that enable a person to make money.

When a person goes after money with the ignorance of what money really is, he will have a wrong mindset towards money and he will not be able to get money but if he gets money such money will come to him with problems because he will be about getting money rather than making money. Money is made and only those who can make money see and enjoy money when they have it. You will also get to understand why this is so as you read on.

The question I believe you are asking which you would want answered at this point is, if the printed paper and stamped coins that are used as legal tender, are only a representation of money, then what is money?

For a clear and easy understanding of what money really is, we will need to take a step backwards in time and see where money is coming from by asking and answering the following questions,

(i) How did money come about?

(ii) Why was money introduced ?

We will also need to ask and answer the question,

whose is money?

How does a person get money?

These questions will assist us in knowing what money really is and how a person should look for it and use it when he has it.

Going by its usage, money can be said to be a means for trading. It is used for commercial transactions. It is used for the payment of goods and services.

However, before the invention and introduction of money in commercial transactions, people used to carry out commercial transactions, they usually do so through trading by batter. I give you my tomatoes and you give me your beans. You give me a goat after I have farmed for you. This practice went on until it became too cumbersome. For example, I have tomatoes and you want it but I don't want your beans. This means we will have to look for someone with what I want, say shoes and the person wants your beans. When this is found the transaction is done but it could happen that we are unable to find someone with what I want or who wants your beans. This means the transaction cannot be done. This was what led to the invention of what we today call money which is a representation of our products or services worth.

Money is therefore VALUE, it is a means for value exchange.

The printed paper and the stamped coins we call money are not value in themselves, they are merely the representation of value which money is. Since the representative of a thing is not the thing and cannot be the thing, it will be wrong for a person to see and go after the printed paper we call money as money. This is why seeing the decorated paper and stamped coins as money is misleading and does not help much especially when it comes to looking for and relating to money.

From what I have explained, it can be said that, when a person has the printed paper or the stamped coins, he is saying that, he has been involved in a transaction which involved the exchange of value which they represent or he has been able to create that much value for society or somebody in the society.

Money is value and one gets it by creating value for others or serving others. A friend of mine says the little pieces of paper and coins we call currency notes and coins are appreciation notes people give us for serving them or creating value for them.

For a person to create value he must have the skills to and so when a person has money he is also saying he has the ability to create that much value.

However, if a person has this printed paper or stamped coins of a certain worth and he has not been involved in the creation and exchanged of that worth of value that they represent then he is a thief. A thief is anyone who has taken something of value that is not his own without giving something of commensurate value in return or exchange.

The world operates on principles or laws that God the creator of the World put in place to control and regulate all things in the world at creation and even though man disobeyed God and handed over the ruler ship of the world to Satan and things are not in the world as God planned them to be, the principles and laws He had put in place to control the world at creation are intact and functioning. A person who steals is a thief and has broken God's law. Just as anyone who breaks a human law gets punished when caught, anyone who breaks any of the laws God has put in place to control things in the World gets punished even if he is not caught. When a person steals, God's law which says, give and get or sow and reap is broken and as such, such a person will end up suffering punishment.

This goes to say that when a person wants money he should

create value and he should never acquire the printed decorated paper and stamped coins without having created value as doing so without this amounts to stealing. Any person who wants money should know this fact and acquire the ability to create value before going after money. How this is done is discussed and explained in details in the chapter that deals with how money is made.

Psalms 24:1-2 and Haggai 2:8 which are quoted below made us to know that money belongs to God ,this means when a person is in the possession of money he is a steward and the money is a trust.

This means money is a responsibility.

Psalms 24:1-2, Says," The earth is the Lord's, and everything in it, the world, and all who live in it; for he founded it upon the seas and established it upon the waters".

Haggai 2:8 says

"The silver is mine and the gold is mine,' declares the Lord Almighty".

24

25

3:00 WHY YOU A CHRISIAN MUST AND SHOULD BE BOTHERED ABOUT MONEY

If you are a Christian then you must and should be interested in the subject of money and must be bothered about it.

This is because,

Money not understood can be a means of distraction by Satan.

The lack of money and inability to relate to money correctly can be a source of stress and a limitation in life.

Money is needed for food which you a Christian cannot live without.

Money is a resource and a means that you will need to carry out the assignment God has given you in the World.

Money is a means for testing character and skills acquisition.

Many of the problems people have in their lives today are caused by money.

Studies about life and the source of problems that people have in their lives confirmed this fact.

These studies revealed that the main reason why most people have money as the source and cause of most of the problems they have in their lives is that they are ignorant about what money really is. Their ignorance of what money really is has resulted in them not being able to handle the subject of money and some main issues of life which are related to money correctly .

Prominent amongst the issues of money which most people have been found to be unable to handle correctly that has made money to become a source and cause of many life problems they have are,

(a) The making of money.

Most people because they are ignorant of what money really is, look for money wrongly

(b) How to correctly relate to and use money.

Most people because they are ignorant of what money is, do not know how to correctly relate to and use money when they acquire it.

It is because of what the ignorance of what money really is and looking for it without having the correct knowledge of what it really is can bring to a person's life that, Paul gave a strong warning to the Church through Timothy about money and the desire to be rich. Paul said, inform the church that, "those who want to be rich and decide to go after money, stand to face many temptations. He said they stand to be trapped by many stupid and harmful desires which can draw them to destruction and ruin."

Speaking further about money Paul warned that, "the love of money is the root of all evils."

It may interest you to know that, the love of money was the door which Satan used to enter into the life of Judas Iscariot and caused him to betray his master, Jesus.

Jesus did also say that a person cannot serve God and money. This means money competes for the soul of man with God.

From all these facts and many others I cannot list here but will be discussed in latter part of this book , we can see and agree that money matters and it is definitely a subject that every Christian should and must be bothered about.

I want you to note that our call to Christians to be bothered about money is not a call for them to WORRY about money ! It is a call for them to be concerned about it and give it attention so that they know all that they need to know about it and be in the position where money will not affect their relationship with God and is unable to hinder them from being who they are supposed to be and doing what they are supposed to do in the World as Christians.

To further stress and make clearer what money really is and the need for Christians and indeed the Church to give attention to money , I will want to discuss and explain in the remaining part of this chapter some more facts about what money really is, the role money can play and not play in a person's life. I will also explain some of the things that money can enable a person to do if he has it and the things money can bring into a person's life if he lacks it or does not have the right attitude towards it.

I am doing this as I said to clarify, stress and make clear why you a Christian must be bothered about money and should not only give it your attention but should also seek to be well educated and informed about it.

When you, a Christian becomes well educated and informed about money, you will know what it really is, whose it is, what role it can play and not play in your life as a Christian in the World and the life to come.

The possession of this knowledge will enable you to know the right attitude you a Christian should have towards money, how you should look for money, how you should use and not use it when you have it.

Money is the one thing that every human including you a Christian will have to interact with daily from the day you were born till the day you leave this World whether you like it or not.

When a person, Christians inclusive, wakes up every day, he is faced with needs that should and must be met for life to be comfortable. Most of these needs are met with things that are purchased with money and so a person has to interact with money or the things bought with money from sunrise to sunset every day whether he likes it or not. If such a person is ignorant of, what money really is, he is unable to make and have adequate supply of it and he is ignorant of the role it can play and not play then he will be in trouble in life as he can become so occupied with the issues of money, especially looking for it that, he can end up spending all his time looking for money. This can lead to unbalanced living which has been found to be a major cause of failure in most people's life.

A friend of mine on coming into the understanding of the importance of money and the role that money plays in life, is fond of saying , "who says money is not important, it is the one thing you cannot avoid while here on earth and even when you are leaving the world it is needed for you to be sent off properly." He says this is because, the coffin you will be put for burial, which is the last thing that you will need will have to be bought with money.

I agree with him and I dare say that money should be on the list of things every Christian must be bothered about and should know about and have.

Money can be likened to air which is a necessity for survival in the world and as such a Christian living in the world cannot neglect money, any Christian who does so will not only not be able to live well but will not finish well in the world.

Money shows up everywhere one turns in the world and in everything one wants to do in the World. It is because of this fact that money has a role to play in all things that the Bible in Ecclesiastes 10:19b says, "money answers everything". This verse is saying money shows up in everything. There is nothing you would want to do in this World that money does not have a part to play directly or indirectly.

The second reason why you a Christian should and must be bothered bout money is the fact that, money has been found to be a major cause of the many problems people have and are living with today which have resulted in them not enjoying their lives. Of all the causes of the problems man faces in life, money ranks right at the top as one of the most important if not the most important cause. For instance, money has been found to be the number one underlying cause of divorce and a threat to emotional harmony in individuals and families. The saying that money cannot buy you happiness is true but you will agree with me that you need to have an adequate quantity of money, to be settled and free to focus on all the aspects of your life that can bring you happiness and joy. When you do not have adequate quantity of money to take care of your needs and that of your family like paying your bills and you are being stressed over how to make ends meet, chances are that you will not only be unhappy but, you will be open to do things that you would not do if not for your lack of money. Your family members will also not be happy, they will feel the tension too. When a person finds himself with financial problems he will be so occupied with how to get money to solve them that he won't be able to do anything else well.

The third reason that I can put forward for why you a Christian must and should be bothered about money is the fact that you need money to be able to live life as it should be lived. You are in the World for a purpose and you will need money to acquire the resources, means, tools, freedom and time to do the things that you should do to fulfill your life purpose.

When a person is preoccupied with financial problems, such a person will usually end up in bondage to money thereby, becoming unable to do any other thing but chase money. With the knowledge of what money really is and how to make money correctly, a person can get money to work for him to earn money for him thereby enabling him to have the freedom and time to do the other things which he needs to do for a fulfilled life but no one can do for him.

Two other reasons that should encourage you a Christian to be bothered about money and should give it attention are that, money is power, it represents a means for dominance and control. Money is to the World what the Holy Spirit is to the Church! Money is the power base of the World hence, while here on earth you need money to have influence. Without money or the ability to call in money when you need it, can result in you not being reckoned with in the World.

Wisdom is good and it is a needed thing in the world but, a man without money, a man who is poor will have his wisdom despised.

Ecclesiastes9:14-15 which I quote below confirms this.

" There was once a small city with only a few people in it. And a powerful king came against it, surrounded it and built huge siege works against it. Now there lived in that city a man poor but wise, and he saved the city by his wisdom. But nobody remembered that poor man".

It is because of this very important role money and riches can play in the world and the life of people while in the world even when they are wise, that God gave King Solomon in addition to wisdom riches(money) when he asked for wisdom when God asked him to ask for what he wants. God gave him riches in addition to wisdom because ,God knew he will need money in addition to his wisdom to be able to live and do what he has been created to do in the world well .Without wealth he could not have been able to function well.

If Christians and indeed the Church could have money and combines it with the power of the Holy Spirit in doing its work in the world especially in the evangelistic effort, it will have a great effect and impact worldwide.

It is because of what this combination of money and the Holy Spirit in the hands of Christians and indeed the church can play in the world that, the world is working hard to keep Christians and the church poor and busy only in the four walls of the church. A church that is involved in commerce and is able to affect and control it and has money is a serious threat the World forces of darkness fear. The world does not fear a spiritual Church that does not threaten commerce and has no money.

The second of these two last reasons that make money a subject that you a Christian must and should be bothered about is the fact that, apart from the fact that you will have to interact with money daily while you are here in the World and there are things that you must do daily which you can do well only when you have money, money will also show up when we get to Heaven. It will show up in where you will spend eternity and what treasures you will have while in heaven. What treasures you will have will be determined by what you did with money while you were here on earth. The Bible is very clear about these facts that, where you will spend eternity and what treasures you will have in heaven will be determined by how you related to money and what you used money for while here on earth. The Bible confirms these truths in the parables found in Matthew 25,

(a)In Matthew 25:1-13 which is quoted below is the parable of the ten virgins. The five foolish virgins ended up outside because they did not invest their money for the purpose for which they were waiting, the arrival of the groom.

In the same vain Christians who will not invest their money into extending the kingdom of God will find themselves outside the kingdom when the end comes.

"At that time the kingdom of heaven will be like ten virgins who took their lamps and went out to meet the bridegroom. Five of them were foolish and five were wise. The foolish ones took their lamps but did not take any oil with them. The wise, however, took oil in jars along with their lamps. The bridegroom was a long time in coming, and they all became drowsy and fell asleep.

"At midnight the cry rang out: 'Here's the bridegroom! Come out to meet him!'

"Then all the virgins woke up and trimmed their lamps. 8 The foolish ones said to the wise, 'Give us some of your oil; our lamps are going out.'

No,' they replied, 'there may not be enough for both us and you.

Instead, go to those who sell oil and buy some for yourselves.'

But while they were on their way to buy the oil, the bridegroom arrived. The virgins who were ready went in with him to the wedding banquet. And the door was shut.

Later the others also came. 'Sir! Sir!' they said. 'Open the door for us!'

But he replied, 'I tell you the truth, I don't know you.'

Therefore keep watch, because you do not know the day or the hour."

The parable of the talents in Matthew 25:14-30 also brings out the fact that how we invest our money will determine where we will spend eternity.

(b)In Matthew 25:31-46 which is quoted below is the parable of the Sheep and Goats. This parable is also telling us what will happen to people as a result of how they use their money while on earth.

The parable says,

"When the Son of Man comes in his glory, and all the angels with him, he will sit on his throne in heavenly glory. All the nations will be gathered before him, and he will separate the people one from another as a shepherd separates the sheep from the goats. He will put the sheep on his right and the goats on his left.

"Then the King will say to those on his right, 'Come, you who are blessed by my Father; take your inheritance, the kingdom prepared for you since the creation of the world. For I was hungry and you gave me something to eat, I was thirsty and you gave me something to drink, I was a stranger and you invited me in, I needed clothes and you clothed me, I was sick and you looked after me, I was in prison and you came to visit me.'

"Then the righteous will answer him, 'Lord, when did we see you hungry and feed you, or thirsty and give you something to drink?

50

When did we see you a stranger and invite you in, or needing clothes and clothe you? When did we see you sick or in prison and go to visit you?'

"The King will reply, 'I tell you the truth, whatever you did for one of the least of these brothers of mine, you did for me.'

"Then he will say to those on his left, 'Depart from me, you who are cursed, into the eternal fire prepared for the devil and his angels. For I was hungry and you gave me nothing to eat, I was thirsty and you gave me nothing to drink, I was a stranger and you did not invite me in, I needed clothes and you did not clothe me,

I was sick and in prison and you did not look after me.'

"They also will answer, 'Lord, when did we see you hungry or thirsty or a stranger or needing clothes or sick or in prison, and did not help you?'

"He will reply, 'I tell you the truth, whatever you did not do for one of the least of these, you did not do for me.'

"Then they will go away to eternal punishment, but the righteous to eternal life."

The GOATS are those who will end up in hell and the reasons given for their ending up in this place are that they did not give food and drink to the hungry, they did not cloth the naked, they did not visit those in prison or sick.

You will agree with me that, for a person to do any of these things listed, the person needs money. If you are to give a hungry person food you will need money to buy the food. If you are a farmer you will need money to acquire the farming implements and the other things needed for farming. If we are to talk of clothing the naked, money is also needed for buying the clothes. Even in visiting the sick or those in prison money is needed for the transport fare if you do not have your car. Even if you have your own car, you will need to buy fuel for the car. Those who did all the things listed, the SHEEP were able to do them and I believe it was because they knew how to get money, got money and used it correctly. It is possible that the GOATS did not have the money because they did not know how to get it or they had it but they chose to use it for other things which they considered as what money should be used for because of their ignorance of what money really is and what should be the right use of money.

From the above facts which I have discussed, you will agree with me that money is indeed a subject that all Christians must and should be bothered about. Christians should and must seek to know, what money really is, how to get it and what the correct use of it is when they get it.

(ii) Mathew 6:19-20 which is quoted below clarifies and confirms the fact that treasures will be needed in heaven so Christians will need to store up for themselves some.

"Do not store up for yourselves treasures on earth, where moth and rust destroy, and where thieves break in and steal. But store up for yourselves treasures in heaven, where moth and rust do not destroy, and where thieves do not break in and steal

It is clear from what this verse says that there will be need for treasures in heaven, hence Jesus advised that we should not lay treasures for ourselves on the

Earth but we should lay them in heaven.

The questions that we will need to answer at these point are ,

(a) how are treasures laid up in heaven by those who are on Earth?

(b) what role does money play in getting this done?

T he answer to the first question is found in Matthew 19:21 which says,

Jesus said to him, "If you want to be perfect, sell what you own .Give the money to the poor, and you will have treasure in heaven."

It is through giving to the poor that a person on earth can lay up treasures in heaven. It is through the giving of things that meet the needs of the poor. These things that are given are definitely bought with money.

These facts are saying that, money is valuable and important as it can be used for doing things which ends up with benefits that accrue to the user while here on earth and in the life to come.

Money has a role to play when it comes to giving as it can be given or it is used for the acquisition of the things that are given. Anyone who would want treasures in heaven will definitely need to bother about money as money is the means by which they are accumulated in heaven.

The following things which amount to roles that money can play or purposes that money can serve or the uses it can be put to as it is related to by people also makes it important and a subject that you a Christian and indeed every Christian must and should be bothered about.

(i) A RESOURCE

Money is a resource which serves many purposes .Prominent amongst these are,

(a) Money is a neutral resource but it takes on the characteristics of its possessor at any given time. Money is therefore a means by which the true nature of a person can be revealed by e.g. if a man is a liar it will be revealed when such a person is involved in money transactions with others. He will lie.

(b)For Carrying out Gods assignments that ,He has given to man on earth either on an individual or corporate level. Money is needed for the acquisition of the materials and tools needed for the execution of the assignment. e.g. money is needed by the church for the acquisition of the equipment etc that are needed for its assignment e.g. evangelism.

(c) Which is needed by Christians for the acquisition of resources they need for sustenance and carrying out of their businesses.

(d) which is used for the payment and exchange for goods and services hence it is referred to as a reward for service and a medium of exchange for goods and services.

(ii)   A MEANS.

Money is a means for,

(a) doing good in the world and earning eternal rewards.

 Christians can use money to do good here in the world and in doing this earn for themselves treasures for life in eternity. This fact is brought out very clearly by what Paul told Timothy in, *1Timothy 6:17-19, which says,*

"Tell those who have riches of this world not to be arrogant and not to place their confidence in anything as uncertain as riches. Instead, they should place their confidence in God who richly provides us with everything to enjoy. Tell them to do good, to do a lot of good things, to be generous, and to share. By doing this they store up a treasure for themselves which is a good foundation for the future. In this way they take hold on eternal life.

What Jesus told the rich young man in

Mark 10:21 also amounts to the same thing Paul told Timothy. He said to the young rich man,

"You're still missing one thing. Sell everything you have. Give the money to the poor, and you will have treasure in heaven."

(b) For training in Stewardship and a determinant of what a person can be trusted with.

Money is a trust from God and as such it is to be stewarded faithfully by all who get it. Money is therefore a means for stewardship training as it is expected that a steward (one who has been given a trust) should be found faithful on the day of accountability.

 1 Corinthians **4:2,which says**,

"Moreover it is required in stewards that one be found faithful." confirms this.

Luke 16:11 which says,

"So if you have not been trustworthy in handling worldly wealth, who will trust you with true riches"

brings out the fact that a person's ability to handle money determines what other forms of wealth or riches God can trust him with.

(c) testing character:

Money in itself is amoral but as we saw earlier, it takes on and reveals the character of the person who has it. It is because of this that money has been referred to or described as "LITMUS PAPER". When you dip Litmus paper in a liquid, you will know whether it is acidic or basic, in the same vein when you place money in a person's hand you will know who he really is. His true character will be revealed. Some people because of this have said there are two conversions and a person must go through the two to be truly converted. They say that there is the conversion of the heart and that of the pocket. Many people have today adapted this and have always said that, a person becomes a true Christian and can live as a true Christian only when these two conversions have actually taken place in his life. A Persons integrity in the handling of financial issues reveals his integrity in the whole of his life. Money is therefore a means of communication, you tell us who you are by how you use your money and what you use your money for.

(d) testing a person's love and care for others, and GOD.

People give money only for what they truly love and care for sincerely. This is why if you want to know what a person really and truly loves and care for, find out what he spends or gives his money on or for. How easily a person gives money away to others or for kingdom projects reveals how much he loves others and how committed he is to GOD. If a person can give money for a thing he can give anything for that thing.

(e) testing if a person has truly repented.

In Luke 3:8 John the Baptist told those who repented that they go and, " bear fruit in keeping with repentance." John specified three areas of their lives. These three areas are where repentance should be expressed and revealed in the life of a person who has repented. These three areas that John said they should bear fruit in are, their social lives (Luke 3:10-11) , their business lives (Luke 3:12-13) and their attitude to money (Luke 3:14). John told them, "Don't extort money and don't accuse people falsely, be content with your pay." A persons attitude towards money reveals whether he has truly repented or not, hence there is this joke that, there are two conversions, that of the heart and that of the pocket.

(iii) POWER

Money is an instrument of power and a form of power and as such a force to be dominated. Creations of God in the world lost their proper relationship with God at the fall and as such they stand to be influenced by invisible realities which man wrestles with in the world. These are the things Apostle Paul in Ephesians6:12, refers to as principalities, powers and authorities.

Ephesians 6:12,For we do not wrestle against flesh and blood, but against powers, against the rulers of the darkness of this age, against spiritual hosts of wickedness in the heavenly places.

Money is one of such. It is being influenced by one of these powers which Jesus Christ referred to as MAMMON.

Mammon energizes money and it gives it a life which makes it very powerful hence money has spiritual power and is able to compete for man's heart with God. The demon behind money is

GREED. Greed manifested in a man's life is destructive and can destroy man. It does this through the passion for the accumulation of material things.

(iv) Money should not be loved.

<u>1 Timothy</u> 6:9-10 which says,

"But people who want to get rich keep falling into temptation. They are trapped by many stupid and harmful desires which drown them in destruction and ruin. Certainly the love of money is the root of all kinds of evil. Some people who have set their hearts on getting rich have wandered from the Christian faith and have caused themselves a lot of grief."

Gives a very important advice and timely warning about money and how to relate to it to all those who would want to embark on the search for money. These verses bring out very clearly the fact that money should not be loved as the love of money is the first step towards all kinds of sins. It says, some people have even turned away from God because of their love for money and as a result they have pierced themselves with many sorrows.

(v) A PERSON SHOULD NOT PUT HIS TRUST IN MONEY

Money is something that a person should not put his trust in.

Many because of being ignorant of what money really is put their trust in money. Such people have been disappointed. .

1 Timothy 6:17 which says,

"command those who are rich in the things of this life not to be proud, and not to put their hope in wealth, which is uncertain, but to put their hope in God who richly provides us with everything for our enjoyment."

And Job 31:24,28 which says,

"If I have put my trust in gold or said to pure gold, you are my security", "then these also would be sins to be judged, for I would have been unfaithful to God on high."

all bring out very clearly the fact that a person should not put his trust in money.

God is the only person that one should and can put his trust in and be sure that He will not change or fail.

(vi) something that a person should not worship.

Money should not be an object of worship. This is so especially for people who wants to worship God. No person can worship God and money.

Luke 16:13 says,

"No servant can serve two masters. Either he will hate the one and love the other, or he will be devoted to the one and despise the other. You cannot serve both God and money."

(vii) TREASURE.

Money is treasure as it is a measure of treasure. This makes money not only important but dangerous as a man's heart can be in it instead of God. A man's heart is where his treasure is.

Matthew 6:21 which says,

Your heart will be where your treasure is. confirms this.

(viii) LIFE

Many have referred to money as life as it is central in the life of man. It is needed for the acquisition of things needed for the sustenance of physical life. It plays a very important role in ensuring that a person has a stable life. Problems in the financial area of a person's life are transmitted to all other areas of his life resulting in such a person not being free and stable to live his life well. It is because of this very important role which money plays and can play in a person's life that money is said to be a defense and it answered all things.

The need for people especially Christians to know what money really is, be able to get it, relate to it correctly and manage it correctly when they get it cannot be over emphasized. It is only when a person understands money and is free from financial bondage that he can be free to live and fulfill his purpose on earth successfully.

Let us conclude this chapter by considering some misconceptions about money which many Christians and indeed the Church as a whole has held unto because of wrong understanding of what money really is and how Christians should relate to it, which have made Christians not to be bothered about money and given it the important attention which they should.

These misconceptions which have made Christians and indeed the church to bother little about money, especially, with the education of Christians about what it really is and how to get and use it, have resulted in them having numerous money problems prominent amongst which is the lack of money. These misconceptions originated from how the gospel has been preached. Over the years, salvation has been the focus of the church and as such the Gospel has been preached and taught as being meant only for the future. Its relevance has been limited to heaven. Evangelists have cried out, "Be saved so that you can make heaven, do not worry about the world and the things of the world." Money is one of the things that they see as a thing of the world and so, Christians were told not to be bothered about it, it is evil.

Let us consider some of these misconceptions that have arisen because of this approach to preaching the gospel and see what the Bible say about them so that Christians will not only know what money really is , eliminate these misconceptions which are clearly the product of ignorance and financial illiteracy to be able to give money the correct and required attention in their lives.

The misconceptions are;

(a)Money is evil and it is the root of all evil.

Many Christians have been taught to see money as evil and as the root of all evil. They usually quote,

1Timothy 6:10 which says,

"Certainly, the love of money is the root of all kinds of evil. some people who have set their hearts on getting rich have wandered away from the Christian faith and have caused themselves a lot of grief."

to buttress their point. This is definitely a misconception as money is not evil and as such not the source of all evils. From what this verse is saying, it is clear that it is the love of money and not money that is the root of all kinds of evil. Money is good and it can be used for many good things when it is in the hands of good people. Christians can do a lot of good in the World if they have money and they will and can be limited if they do not have money.

(b) Money corrupts and as such rich people will not go to heaven.

Many Christians interpret **Matthew 19:23** which says,

Jesus said to His disciples, "I can guarantee this truth: It will be hard for a rich person to enter the kingdom of heaven. I can guarantee again that it is easier for a camel to go through the eye of a needle than for a rich person to enter the kingdom of God."

to mean that rich people will not go to heaven. This means all rich people will go to hell. This is not true as Luke 16:19-26 which I quote below reveals that Abraham who was very rich is in heaven. It is therefore possible to be rich and holy. The rich man in hell did not go to hell because he was rich, he did because of who he was and how he lived while on earth.

"There was a rich man who was dressed in purple and fine linen and lived in luxury every day. At his gate was laid a beggar named Lazarus, covered with sores and longing to eat what fell from the rich man's table. Even the dogs came and licked his sores. The time came when the beggar died and the angels carried him to Abraham's side. The rich man also died and was buried. In hell, where he was in torment, he looked up and saw Abraham far away, with Lazarus by his side. So he called to him, 'Father Abraham, have pity on me and send Lazarus to dip the tip of his finger in water and cool my tongue, because I am in agony in this fire. But Abraham replied, 'Son, remember that in your lifetime you received your good things, while Lazarus received bad things, but now he is comforted here and you are in agony. And besides all this, between us and you a great chasm has been fixed, so that those who want to go from here to you cannot, nor can anyone cross over from there to us."

(c)Money is a worldly thing.

Talking about money to Christians is not only wrong and not necessary but it will amount to encouraging materialism and so it should not be done.

Many have said money is worldly and as such getting Christians to be bothered about it is encouraging materialism and worldliness. This claim is wrong and as such a misconception because,

the things that are said to constitute worldliness do not include money. They are lust of the eye, lust of the flesh and the pride of life.

materialism is living unto and for material possessions which are associated with money because money is used for their acquisition. Educating Christians about money to know what it really is, how to get it, how to relate to it and what to use it for, amounts to educating them about materialism thereby enabling them to know what money and material things can do for them and what they cannot do. This will enable them to develop the right attitude towards them. People who are victims of greed and materialism are usually people who are ignorant of what money and material things really are, what they can do and not do and the right way to relate to them.

4:00 YOU A CHRISTIAN AND FINANCIAL SUCCESS

Given what money is, the role it can play and what it can be used for, I dare say that financial success is one success that you a Christian should desire and must seek to achieve.

Before we can say yes or no to this claim, I think we should ask and answer the question,

WHAT IS FINANCIAL SUCCESS?

Most people see and define, financial success as being in the possession of plenty or large sums of money. They associate financial success with the concept of "having made it in life" which is usually looked at as having acquired and being in the possession of large sums of money. Most people therefore think that the achievement of financial success is about having money and as such they will consider themselves or a person successful financially only when they or such a person has a lot and enough money resulting in such a person no longer lacking money. Financial success to these people is measured only in terms of the quantity of money that a person has.

This definition of financial success is wrong as the conditions described by the definition are not attainable by a human being. It is not possible for a person to have enough money or arrive at always having money to do whatever he wants to do when he wants to do it and not lacking money.

It may surprise you to hear this but, the truth is that financial success has nothing to do with the quantity of money and as such the achievement of true financial success by a person is not about the quantity of money such a person has.

A person's level of financial success is measured by his level of financial freedom and financial independence.

Financial freedom has to do with freedom from financial bondage. A person's level of financial freedom is therefore measured by how free the person is from financial bondage. Being in bondage to a thing is about being a slave to the thing and how much a person is being limited or controlled by the thing and so financial freedom has to do with how free a person is from the control of money. It is measured by how much a slave to money a person is. How free a person is from money and how much a slave a person is to money is measured or revealed by the person's behavior when it comes to money and money issues.

It is about how much money influences his behavior.

Financial independence on the other hand has to do with a

person knowing what money really is and possessing the ability to be able to earn money, such that he is able to do what can earn him money whenever he needs money. Such a person is free from depending on others for money.

A person's level of financial success is therefore determined by the person's attitude towards money and his abilities when it comes to earning money .

The attainment of financial success by Christians is important and necessary; this is because a Christian that is not financially successful is never free to be able to live and fulfill his purpose in the World.

Did I hear you ask why?

It is because a Christian that is not financially successful will be in financial bondage.

The next question I think we should answer is, what is being in financial bondage all about and why are Christians that are in financial bondage not able to live and fulfill their purpose in the World?

Being in bondage to a thing results in being a slave to the thing and because being a slave to a thing means being under the total control of the thing, a person in bondage to a thing will be unable to function as he should.

A Christian in financial bondage will be a slave to money and will not be free to do any other thing well. He will live for money and will be controlled by money. All his decisions will be determined by money.

Studies have revealed that a person in financial bondage will have financial difficulties that can result in the person being unable to live and do any other thing well in life.

Some of the things that a person in financial bondage will exhibit are as follows,

(i) **Worry over money and money matters-** when a person lives with anxiety over money and money issues, he will end up in financial bondage.

(ii) Greed- a person is greedy when such a person's life is characterized by wanting things. Wanting the biggest, the best or things others have. Such a person will be in financial bondage.

(iii) Anger - when a person is angry over what others have and he does not have he will be in financial bondage.

(iv) Resentment- when a person is in the habit of blaming others for his financial situation and does not take responsibility for his condition. Such a person is in financial bondage.

(v) Self Indulgence - when a person is in the habit of buying things that are with little or no utility he will end up in financial bondage.

(vi)Poor record keeping when it comes to finance-when a person is not able to keep accurate records for his finances and does not live by a budget he will not be a faithful steward of money. Such a person will end up in financial bondage.

The existence of these financial difficulties and problems in a person's life are however symptoms of underlying problems in the person's life. These problems are usually spiritual. When a person's spiritual life is not in order, such a person will have problems show up in all dimensions of his life especially the financial dimension.

The underlying problems that lead a person into being in financial bondage include the following,

(i) Financial ignorance

If you lack knowledge about finances, especially what God's word says about money and stewardship, you will end up with financial difficulties.

(ii) Wrong attitude towards material things

If your attitude towards material things is that of lack of contentment and you are always wanting to gather things then be careful as you will end up with financial difficulties as this attitude is not the attitude of a Godly steward it is the attitude of greed which is not godly.

(iii) Poor planning

Operating without a financial plan will keep you in financial bondage as you will have no guide for your behavior when it comes to money and its usage. A financial plan is a means for guiding and modifying a person's financial behavior. A financial budget is an important aspect of a financial plan which controls financial behavior.

5:00 WHAT YOU A CHRISTIAN NEED TO BE ABLE TO ACHIEVE FINANCIAL SUCCESS

From what we saw as the definition of financial success in the last chapter, what do you think a Christian needs to be able to achieve financial success?

From the last chapter it is clear that the achievement of financial success by a person is not about such a person having large sums of money but it is rather about,

The person being free from the control of money such that his behavior and decisions in all situations is not influenced by money. He is able to take decisions and relate to people without reference to money at all times.

(ii) the person having the knowledge and skills needed to make money correctly.

Studies have revealed that, a person's behavior at any given time or in a given situation or as regards any given matter and what he can do at any given time or in any given situation or matter are determined by his attitudes and skills while, a person's attitudes and skills are a product of his, knowledge, beliefs, values, goals, ability to control himself and do rightly what he is expected to do at any given time and training.

The life plan and strategy that such a person lives by have also been found to be determinants of how such a person behaves in a given situation or carries out an activity.

It can therefore be said that, the achievement of financial success by a person is dependent on such a person's attitude towards money and his behavior in money matters. However, since these are determined by,

his knowledge about money and money matters (financial literacy).

his values in life.

beliefs about money.

goals especially in the area of money.

how patient and disciplined such a person is when it comes to money and money matters

Such a person's life plan . A life plan comprises a financial plan and it can modify and guide a person's financial behavior as a financial plan incorporates a person's values, vision, goals, strategies and activities for making and managing money. A life plan is therefore a necessity for all those who would want to achieve financial success.

From the above, it can be said that who a person is, character wise, his level of financial literacy, the possession of attributes and skills that can enable him to discipline, organize and manage himself to work, create and trade value rightly and profitably and then steward the money he makes through doing this faithfully, determines his potential for achieving financial success.

The questions that we will need to answer here to be able to know what a Christian needs to be able to achieve financial success are,

(a) Who does a Christian(a born again person) need to become to have all the character traits and attributes needed for doing all the things listed above rightly?

(b) What are the skills that such a person needs for him to be able to correctly create and trade value to correctly earn and faithfully steward money for him to be able to achieve financial success?

It has been discovered that a Christian will have to become GODLY to have these character traits and attributes. Only a GODLY Christian has the character traits and attributes that can enable a person to achieve financial freedom, the first requirement for the achievement of true financial success .

Such a person is able to achieve financial freedom because, becoming a Godly person enables a person to have a pure heart and is able to be free from the control of money and being in financial bondage. Such a person will not be greedy, love money or put his trust in money.

Being Godly and having Godly character traits only enables a person to be able to achieve financial freedom and this is not all that a person needs to achieve financial success.

For a person to achieve financial success he will need to also become financially independent. For financial independence he will need to acquire financial literacy (knowledge of money), productive and commercial skills that with his pure heart he can create and trade value with love and profitably. He will also need money management skills. These will enable him to faithfully steward the money he makes.

From all that I have explained above, the steps a person who wants to achieve financial success must follow are as follows,

(i) The person must first become a true Christian by being born again.

(ii) He must have his mind renewed.

Having these two things in place will enable him to become a Godly person and have the character traits and attributes that can enable him to be able to achieve financial freedom.

Mind renewal enables such a person to acquire a wealthy

mindset, a requirement that a person must have to come out of poverty. Having this mindset determines whether a person can overcome poverty or not as it changes how people see themselves. How a person sees himself is the main determinant of who such a person can be. It is because of this that without a wealthy mindset a person can never become wealthy. Such a person can't see himself wealthy and as such he cannot create and trade value profitably.

(iii) He will have to,

(a) become financially literate by becoming knowledgeable about money.

(b) acquire skills for making and stewarding money faithfully.

A Christian who knows and is able to acquire all the things listed above can achieve true financial success because being financially literate and possessing these requirements bestow on him the three things a person needs to become a person who can carry out an endeavor successfully.

The three things that a person needs to carry out an endeavor successfully are commitment, competence and capacity.

I will however want to go further to explain these requirements that a Christian needs for the achievement of financial success.

Studies have revealed that many people know the principles of making money but when it comes to coming up with what to do to apply these principles they are usually left in the dark, they do not know the ways that money is made.

For the sake of these people I have discussed and explained in the next four chapters,

the ways of making money.

what a Christian needs to be able to live and make money in the World.

how a Christian should live and look for money.

How a Christian should use the money he makes.

A case study on how the Church should enable its members to overcome money lack.

I believe discussing and explaining these things will make how a Christian should live and make money in the world and relate to it correctly clear.

It is my hope that discussing these things will enable you a Christian to have a complete knowledge of what you need to know, have and be able to do to achieve financial success and be free from financial bondage.

109

6:00 EXPLANATION OF HOW MONEY IS MADE AND THE WAYS OF MAKING MONEY

The World is a cause and effect place and as such nothing happens without it being caused. Things are caused before they happen, a person can therefore get anything only after it has to been caused. In the same vein when it comes to making money it is required that a person will have to cause money to flow to him before he can get money. A person can therefore make money only if he can cause money to flow to him by doing what enables money to be released to a person.

The implication of the above truth is that, there are ways for causing a particular thing to happen and so, for a person to make money, he must know and apply correctly the ways of making money before he can make it.

Money is value and as such, a person can live in the World and make money only if he is able to live create and trade value profitably. There are four main ways by which a person can live and create value and make money. These four ways by which a person can live, create and trade value profitably are the known ways by which a person can make money while in the world. These four ways are the ways that people have been using over the years to make money and they are the ways that will ever be used. They unlock the secrets to getting money. Any person who wants to get money, Christian or non Christian must know and apply them to make money.

I will in the remaining part of this chapter discuss and explain these four ways of making money. I have explained what they are and how they enable their users to make money. The chapter closes with how you a Christian should live and apply these ways of making money to get money. It explains how a Christian should live and use any or all the ways of making money to make money correctly.

The four main ways of making money are,

- Employment
- Business
- Investing
- Invention/Intellectual property development

Whoever you are and where ever you live in the World, if you want to make money, you will have to know these four ways of making money and the principle behind each method and apply them for you to be able to make money.

It has been found that in all of human history these are basically the only genuine main ways for making money. All other ways are hybrids of these .Four is not very many but a person will not need to use all four at any given time to be able to make money as he can make money using any one of the four at any given time. This means you can choose and use any one of the ways that you understand the principle behind and competent to apply or use at any one time and use it to make money.

There are people who have however become wealthy, interestingly through using all four methods at the same time. I will however advise that before you embark on wanting to use all the ways at the same time to make money, make sure that you have the capacity and ability.

The details of each method or way and how they enable a person who uses them to make money are as follows,

(i) Employment

The first way that a person can use to make money is, by being employed by another, this involves working for another person.

Work enables a person to create and exchange value. Value that a person creates meet the need of people and as such someone pays for it. The payment that a person gets is reward for his work or labor.

Now, the question that I want to ask you is, why on

earth do you think anyone would employ you and pay you to work for him?

Why would they give you money if you work for them? Think about that for a minute.

Why would anybody pay you to work for him?

Why wouldn't they just do it themselves and keep their money?

Studies have revealed that they will do it because what you are doing as work for them is something that, either they can't do or they don't want to do or they can't get someone else to do it for them better or cheaper than you.

This means, when you work, you are rewarded for doing things that other people, don't want to do or can't do or someone can't do better or cheaper!

Get this deep into your mind; capture it, because it is the principle of work and making money that you must know and understand if you want to be able to make money by working for other people.

Most people don't understand this principle of work and making money.

The only condition you can continue to be paid by a person for what you do for him is if what you do for him is something that he can't do, doesn't want to do or can't get any other person to do it for him better or cheaper.

This is simply saying to you that you have three ways that you can get employed and paid to work for somebody. These are, *find what people, can't do or don't want to do or can't find another to do for them cheaper or better.*

What this is saying is that you stand to get paid and paid more for what you do or can do as work if your work enables you to do for your employer or others what he or they cannot do, does not want to do or can't find someone else to do for him or them cheaper and better.

If there is a job in your community that nobody wants to do or the owners can't do or there is no one doing it, train yourself to do it as this is work which you can get paid well to do.

A very good example of this is disposal of waste. If you go to an advanced nation with a well developed economy, waste disposal people make lots of money. Become a waste disposer in a country like the United States and you will make a lot of money. They will pay you well to do it, this is all because most people do not want to be waste collectors and disposers in the United States.

This brings me to another important point. If you are to do either something that people don't want to do or something that they can't do, which do you think will enable you to get paid more? The "can't do" jobs, the one the people can't do I believe. Why do you think this is so ?

It is because if it is what they can't do, and can't find another easily to do better or cheaper then you stand to get to tell them how much it is going to cost them and they will pay as they have no choice , but if it is what they can do but don't want to do and the amount that you quote is too high, they will make time to do it themselves even if it is something they don't like to do. But if it is something they can't do, then they will have no choice but to plead and negotiate with you.

This means you get paid more for doing things that others can't do and can't find others to do than for doing things that others just don't want to do but can do.

What creates economic value is scarcity.

Scarcity is the source of economic value!

There is lots of sand in the world, and hence it's not very expensive while, there are not very many diamonds hence they are special and are very expensive.

Sand and diamonds are both useful, but there's not very many of diamond and hence it's much more expensive. So, be a diamond when it comes to what you do or can do as work instead of sand which can be found everywhere and easily.

It is therefore better to be a diamond than sand when it comes to the work you can do as you can make a lot more money through being able to do work that not too many can do than the one there are many who can do .

Even in the area of skill development, this also apply. When it comes to selecting the skill to acquire or develop, select a skill that is not readily available. Develop skills that are not possessed by many people but are needed. This will enable you to be in the position to do what not too many people can do. Consider for an example the case below which is a testimony from somebody in Nigeria about what I have discussed above. He selected and learned Arabic in addition to English as a third language when he and his schoolmates were learning English as a second language. He did this when he saw that there were many oil companies from America working in Arabic countries and they have need for people who can speak both English and Arabic but not many people who can do this were available. He reasoned that anyone who can, will be needed by these oil companies to help them to talk with the locals and will be paid lots of money to do it.

This is his testimony, read it and you will understand what I have been trying to explain above. "I came from a poor family and as such had to go to work early. I started to work at a very early age to survive. All the other students in my class were studying English and French when we were in the secondary school. So I started studying English and Arabic. I learned to speak English and Arabic and in 1980, when I finished my secondary school moved to Saudi Arabia. There were not very many people who could speak both Arabic and English there then. This ability was scarce so it was valuable. I was able to get a job at a major oil company and even though I was just a secondary school leaver, I was paid almost three times as much as a University graduate. This happened because I could do something they couldn't do. " Let me also tell you of yet another case of a person who was able to earn a lot of money through work he can do because he possesses a unique skill which enables him to do what others can't do."I used to live in a house near a gentleman who had a very unique skill. He could play football. There aren't very many people who could do this as he could, kick around this round leather thing. Now even though there is no intrinsic value in being able to kick around this round thing, as far as I am concerned, this gentleman is paid a lot of money every year for kicking around this round thing.

He has a particular skill and can do things that other people can't do. What i am saying here is that if you have a skill that very few other people have, you can make lots of money working for others with it?

From what I have discussed above, one may think that all a person needs to be able to make a lot of money through working for others is to have a unique skill which enables him to do what others don't want to do or can't do, but studies have revealed that this is not enough. A person will need in addition other qualities as the reward for work is always based on the motive for doing the work, the quantity of the work done and the quality of the work done. So, you can work very hard and make a lot of money and become rich with work as your means of making money only if you do it for the right reason, with the right motive and a positive mental attitude. This means that you have to do work for the right reason, be happy at work and happy doing it. Permit me to bring in yet another testimony to clarify how the aspect of quantity, quality and attitude applies and affect money making, "I started of as a speaker when speaking fees were not much. Little organizations with a few staff would have me speak to their staff. Then I got invited to speak at larger meetings/conferences to larger groups and that enabled me to earn more. Now, I get up to one hundred thousand naira to speak for an hour and to bigger organizations. My average audience has increased making me able to serve many more people resulting in me earning more, much more than when I started. The value of work and what is paid for it is determined by the reason for, quantity and quality of the work. You get paid exceedingly well and you stand to be blessed by what you are paid for your work if the reason for your work is right and its quantity and quality are high.

If you work with or for the right reason and with a good attitude, not only do you feel good but everyone around you feels good too. Whenever we organize our workshop in a church, the church leadership always make comments about our passion. Why do you think this is so? It is because of our attitude .

Attitude is the multiplier effect that gets added on to the work that a person does when engaged in doing things that people can't do or don't want to do that makes it more valuable and attracts more pay.

(ii) Business

This is the second way of making money. This is one way of making money that you will need to pay a lot of attention to, as you seek to know how to make money.

If you look at most of the truly wealthy people in the world, you will find out that this is how most of them got there. Most of them were not workers, although there are a few people who get rich that way. That is not where the bulk of wealth comes from. The bulk of wealth in the world comes from business.

Think of three or four billionaires who immediately come to mind. What are their names, and how did they get there? If you do, the picture will instantly become clearer to you . Are you thinking of Bill Gates in the United States, yes, he got there by building a business. Are you thinking of Dangote in Nigeria, yes, he got there by building a business.

What really is business and does it enable a person to make money ? I am wearing a shirt as I write this book so, I will want us to use the process of having a shirt made to explain what business is and how it is used for making money.

If you want a shirt made for you, you will have to buy the material, the thread, the buttons and you can pay a tailor to do the sewing. The question is how much do you pay him and how do you determine how much to pay him. In calculating and fixing what to pay the tailor you must allow for a profit for him. Did I hear you ask what is profit and why do you have to allow for profit for him? Why should there be any profit left over? Many people are not able to answer these questions. This is because most people do not understand what business is all about and what profit really is in a business and why a business should make profit. This ignorance exist because why there should be a profit left over is not taught and explained in business schools or business books that have been written .So let me again ask you the reader, what is profit and why do you think there should be any profit left over in a business transaction like the one I described above? Most of us in business know how to calculate profit, but we do not know really what it is and why there should be any in business transactions?

For us to understand why there should be a profit left over to the tailor who produces the shirt we will need to analyze and understand what goes into the production of the shirt. We will need to take a look at what a business transaction is and what is paid for. A business transaction is all about the creation and trading of value. For value to be created work and organization have to be done. It is therefore this work and organization which goes in for the creation of value that are paid for in a business transaction. For our example, it is what goes in as work and organization before a shirt is produced that is paid for. There is a lot of organization needed before a shirt is produced and so, even though you want a shirt you may not want to spend the time to organize all that is needed to produce a shirt.

What this tells us is that profit is the reward of organization. That is the important thought you need to capture here. **Profit is the reward for organization.**

So, if you organize things that other people don't want to organize or cannot organize, they will allow you to keep a profit at the end of every purchase as your reward for doing that.

Let me take some time and give you a short run on business

management. Given what business is all about and what a business person is paid for, what do you think a person in business should concentrate on when he goes into business? Should he be about producing the product or rendering the service his business produces or renders? None of these, yes none of these as concentrating on any of these makes such a person a worker and not a business person. This is how people make money using what we saw as number one way of making money.

So is his job to take the risk of the business? The answer is No. That will be the third way of making money which is called INVESTING, it is what we will discuss next. It is the investor who should be taking the risk.

So ,when you are in business, what is your job? What do you do? It is to ORGANIZE! You are to bring together diverse resources and diverse talents to create a value that can only be produced with organization.

When you travel by air, will you want to have to organize the plane and have the airplane available to take off? You would have to have permission to take off, have a flight plan, pilots to fly the plane. You need an engineer to look after all the equipment, a navigator, stewardesses to serve the meals. You have to have somebody cater the meals. You have to have somebody handle the baggage. How many of you would want to have to handle all these every time you have to fly? None I believe.

This is why we are happy to pay the airlines to do it. If they organize it well, they can receive profit at the end of the day as the reward of their organization.

Business is therefore all about organization and a business person gets paid for organization. How about that for a business management class even though we are about how to make money!

(iii) Investing

The third way that you can make money is to invest.

You can get paid very well through investing. The question is, what is investing and when you invest, what is it that you get paid for? where should a person invest?

If you are not able to answer these questions you can't make a success of investing.

    To invest simply means to deploy money for profit and what you get paid for when you invest is RISK.

In investing, you get rewarded for the risk that you take!

You get paid for taking a risk that somebody either doesn't want to take or can't take.

So, let me ask, when you put your money in the bank, are you taking a risk? The answer is, Yes.

How does a person know this? How do you know that there is risk when you put money in the bank? There is risk in putting your money in the bank because they pay you!

If there were no risk, you would have to pay them for watching over your money. But they pay you interest for putting money in the bank, because they loan your money out to other people as they don't want to take the risk of loaning their own money. Bankers are very smart. They take your money and loan it to somebody else and they collect interest from the people to whom they loan the money; and they pay interest (less than they collect) to you and keep the difference. They are willing to pay you for taking the risk. The interest rate they pay you is low because the risk is not very high.

What we often get taught about investing is that you should minimize your risk. Now, risk is the only thing that you are getting paid for when you invest so this advice is wrong. If you minimize your risk when investing, you are minimizing your reward!

I want you to note this principle about investing that if you minimize your risk, you minimize your reward, it is what every investor must know.

What you really want to do in investing is maximize your risk. You want to maximize the risk that you get paid for taking by taking risks that are easy for you to take but difficult for others.

Not every risk is equal, there are some risks that I am very willing to take that you might not be willing to take. If a lot of other people don't want to take that risk, but I do then, I can get paid a lot of money for assuming that risk if the investment turns in good returns.

This means for a person to make money through investing he will need to find types of risks that he can specialize in. Then he will want to take as much of this type of risk as possible, so that he gets paid as much as possible when he invests.

For success in investing what a person needs to do for success is to find an area of risk where he enjoys a competitive advantage.

The question that we will need to ask and answer before closing this section is ,where can one invest and what should a person use as criteria for selecting an investment opportunity?

This question can be answered in one sentence, invest in an opportunity only if the opportunity enables you to produce a product or render a service that solves a human problem or meet a human need. Invest only the amount that you can afford to lose. Many people have lost their monies for activities that were sold to them as investment opportunities when they were PONZI or PYRAMID schemes. Ponzi and pyramid schemes are scams and not investment opportunities as they do not have a product or service that either solves a problem for people or meet a human need.

(iv) Intellectual Property

The fourth way for making money is intellectual property development. This is where you get paid for THINKING.

When you create intellectual property, you get paid for thinking.

The greatest riches in all history are made from method number four — INTELLECTUAL PROPERTY which is about thinking.

Writing a book is intellectual property development. If you can write a book, and you are able to publish through a publisher you stand to get royalties. Through this you get paid not once but you get paid again and again and again and again. We call this "money while you sleep." When you are able to do this you end up literally having a money tree. Your books can sell all over the world bringing you money from all over the world.

One of the things that you can sell as intellectual property is a process. A computer program is a process. An invention is an intellectual property. A song is an intellectual property. A play is an intellectual property.

In the music industry, we see musicians on the stage performing songs and selling records, but sometimes a percentage of the income they make goes to the person who wrote the song they sing.

Some of you are familiar with a country music star by the name Dolly Parton. Dolly Parton I learnt wrote the song, I WILL ALWAYS

LOVE YOU, but she didn't sing it. Whitney Houston sang it when she was alive. This song is said to have been the only song in history ever to have been the number one song of the year for two years in a row. Dolly Parton is still laughing about it. When asked about the song and how it has performed since Whitney sang it, she said, "I am really glad that I let Whitney sang it. I don't have to go on stage." Dolly Parton doesn't have to perform in a concert to make money with that song. She doesn't have to travel around the world singing the song to make money with it, but because she wrote it, every time that song is played on the radio, every time Whitney had a concert and sang it, every time it is downloaded on iTunes, she is paid money and all she had to do was compose the song using her song writing skill which is a value creation skill!

This is about working once and being paid for life as long as what you produced when you worked remains relevant and useful. If you write it or invent it, you can get paid forever. This is what earning money from intellectual property development is all about.

There are other ways of making money which many people have used to make money which I have left out. I have left them out because they do not represent ways of making money, they are rather ways of getting money. There is a big difference between making money and getting money.

When money comes to a person as a result of his having created and traded value, he is said to have made money but when money comes to a person without having created and traded value he is said to have gotten money. These other ways I have not discussed are ways by which people have money flow to them without creating value.

This book has been written to teach people especially Christians the correct ways of making, relating to and using money and as such these other ways do not belong here as we do not approve of them as correct ways of causing money to flow to a person.

These other ways that I have left out include, gambling ,stealing and patronizing get rich quick approaches for making money! Many people have made a lot of money through these methods but such people have ended up with many problems in their lives.

These people have ended up with problems because these approaches violate God's principle of you must give before you get and as such any money that a person is able to have flow to him through using any of these methods will not be a blessing from God. Only God's blessings can make a person rich and will not bring him sorrows hence any money "made" using these methods ends up bringing problems to their users.

I do not approve of them as they are not ways Christians can use to make money hence they have not been discussed and explained as a way of making money.

Many people have fallen victims of these wrong ways of making money because of their ignorance of what money is and how it should be made especially by Christians. I will therefore want to bring the discussions about, how to make money to a close with this word of advice, if you want to make money, never patronize any money making method which does not enable you to produce a product or render a service which is beneficial to people. If you do, you may make money but such money will bring to you sorrows and will not be a blessing to you.

153

7:00 THINGS THAT YOU A CHRISTIAN MUST AND SHOULD KNOW, HAVE AND BE ABLE TO DO, TO BE ABLE TO LIVE AND MAKE MONEY IN THE WORLD.

For you a Christian to be able to live and make money using any of the ways by which money is made in the World there are things you must know, have and be able to do.

The possession of these things enables you to have what we call the "three c's" for making money. For a person to be able to do anything, making money inclusive, he must have the three C's

For details of what the three C's are, why a person needs them to be able to do things and how they are acquired you may wish to read the authors book titled, THE THREE CEES AND AN S.

The three C's are, commitment, competence and capacity.

PROMINENT AMONGST THE THINGS THAT YOU A CHRISTIAN MUST,

 (a)KNOW to be able to live and make money are,

There are things you a Christian must know about money and the world to be able to live in the world and make money.

To be able to live and make money a Christian needs to know the following things about money and the World,

(i) Nobody is born with money so money is made or earned while in the world.

(ii) The world is controlled by laws or principles and as such things are accessed through obeying the laws and principles that control them.

An example of the laws that control access to things in the world is the law of cause and effect.

(iii) Money is value and so it is caused through the creation of value. For a person to be able to cause money to flow to him he will have to create value. As we saw earlier anyone who gets money without creating value is a thief and such a person stands to suffer consequences of being a thief.

(iv) Value is created through work. Work enables a person to create value for people, but for a person to work and create value such a person needs a means for value creation. This means for value creation can either be a job, business, an intellectual property or an investment. For a person to work he needs the skills to carry out or operate the means for value creation.

(v) Despite the fact that money is made or earned through value creation, it is not earned or made once a person can create value especially by a Christian. This is because, money is not free for the taking by those who want it in the World and can find what to do to create value for others. Money is under control and access to it is controlled even when a person can create value. I t is because of this that it is not those who are working hard that have money.

Money is under the control of God and Satan and they are the givers of money. They determine who gets money in the world. They give only to those that are theirs (Citizens of their kingdom) who ask through the creation of value and obeys the principles that control money.

(vi) Satan does not want Christians to have money and so, when a Christian ask for money through finding , creating and operating a means for creating value(this is either a job, business or investment) and obeys the laws of money, Satan works to make sure that the means does not yield money to the Christian. Satan is able to do this when he can get access into the Christians life to steal what the Christian earns, kill him to stop him from operating the means of value creation he has created or by destroying the means of value creation as a whole.

This is why for a Christian the making of money does not start and end with having the skills for creating value and the means for creating value. To be able to live and make money in the world a Christian will need in addition to these two skills to become a person who is protected from Satan by God and must have a means of value creation that is also protected from Satan by God. Such a means is bless able by God.

A Christian and his means of value creation will have to be inaccessible and remain inaccessible to Satan and bless able by God always for him to be able to live and make money. For details of how to find, select, create and operate successfully a value creation means, you may wish to get a copy of the author's book titled, THE BOOK YOU MUST READ BEFORE STARTING YOUR OWN BUSINESS.

(vii) Money is given to a Christian by God but it is not given as a gift. Money like all other things that God gives man is A TRUST and so the requirement for seeing more of it when a person is given it is faithful stewardship.

A Christian who cannot steward money faithfully will not see much money. What faithful stewardship is and how it is done for a Christian to be termed faithful are discussed in the chapter, HOW YOU A CHRISTIAN SHOULD USE MONEY WHEN YOU MAKE IT.

(b)HAVE to be able to live and make money in the world include,

(i)For a Christian to be able to live and make money in the world he will need to have things that can enable him to become a person who can live and act rightly in life and especially when it comes to making money.

For us to know what these things that you a Christian must have are, we will need to know what it means to act rightly when it comes to money matters and what making money correctly is,

A person is said to act correctly when it comes to money matters when he acts based on God's principles, so money is said to have been correctly made when it is made in a Godly way. A Godly way of doing a thing is when the thing is done following or in line with God's principles.

The correct way of making money is therefore making money using God's principles.

First on the list of these requirements that a Christian must have for making money correctly is therefore, having the things that enables him to become a Godly person with Godly character traits. Such a person is able to live and do things in a Godly way. It is only by the possession of these character traits and lifestyle that such a person can live and make money correctly. I believe you are not surprise by what I have said here. This requirement is necessary for those who call themselves Christians because not everyone who has accepted Jesus Christ as his savior and calls himself a Christian is Godly and has Godly character traits and lifestyle. There are many who have given their lives to Jesus Christ but are carnal and live carnally. Becoming Godly and possessing Godly character traits which enables a person to have a Godly lifestyle requires mind renewal.

Mind renewal brings about the total transformation of a person hence, it is necessary for Godly behavior and lifestyle which are needed by a Christian to be able to live and make money correctly.

Many who call themselves Christians are unable to live make and manage money correctly and it is all because they have un renewed minds and as such are untransformed. The possession of a Godly character and the attributes associated with it are foundational requirements needed by a Christian to be able to live, make money correctly, have the right attitude towards it and manage or use it correctly. Being Godly and possessing Godly character traits form the foundational requirement a Christian must have for making money because they enable a person to have a wealthy mindset and a heart for true service which is a very important necessity for making money. Without a wealthy mindset and a true heart for service a person cannot create and trade value correctly and make money correctly. A Christian that is Godly and has Godly character traits will live by a Godly lifestyle. This will enable such a Christian to have the protection and partnership of God in all that he is involved in. Being a Godly Christian with Godly character traits also enables a Christian to have the capacity to be able to receive, contain and use money correctly without such a person losing his senses. When a person gets money and he does not have the capacity to receive, contain and use it correctly, he can go "burst" just as a balloon that has gotten more air than it can carry put into it goes burst.

These two requirements are therefore foundational and critical for any Christian who wants to make money. They make up the first group of requirements that a person who is a Christian must have to be able to live in the World and make money, have it and also have peace of mind. This is because the money such a person makes does not bring him sorrow as it is a product of God's blessing.

The second group of requirements that a Christian who wants to live and make money correctly must have are made up of things which their lack have been found to be the reason why many Godly people have remained poor financially.

These things include;

(i)KNOWLEDGE

He must have knowledge about,

(a) Money.

Knowledge about money is called financial literacy. A Christian must be financially literate to be able to live and make money in the World. The lack of knowledge is a destroyer of people in all dimensions of life hence the Bible in Hosea 4:6 says people are destroyed for lack of knowledge.

(b) the world.

A Christian who wants to live and make money in the World must have the correct knowledge of how the world sees Christians and what the world's relationship with Christians really is. He will also need to have the correct knowledge of how this relationship affects Christians access to things especially money, in the world.

(c) Skills

A Christian who wants to live and make money in the World must have the following skills sets,

(i) Self management.

(ii) Service (value creation).

(iii) Relationships (creation and sustenance),

(iv) Faithful stewardship.

Without these requirements a Christian cannot live, make and use money correctly in the World.

Because of the importance and necessity of these requirements for making and managing money correctly and by extension the achievement of financial success, I will want to use the remaining part of this chapter to discuss and explain each of them in details.

Let us start the discussion with the first of these things that all Christians who want to make money must have.

I. Knowledge

The Bible in Hosea 4:6 says people perish for lack of knowledge. This means that a person will suffer in the area of life he lacks knowledge. Christians lack knowledge in the area of money and the world they live in hence they are perishing in this area. To perish means to suffer. So when Christians lack knowledge about money and how to get things in the world they live in they will perish or suffer in the area of money and in their ability to get things in the world . What Christians need to know to be able to live and make money in the world include the following,

II. In the World things, money inclusive are given, they are not available freely for whoever wants to go out and get as much as he wants.

The ignorance of this truth has been found to be responsible for why many Christians are laboring wrongly as they look for money. God used an event I saw as I sat in my mechanics workshop and waited for my car to be repaired to illustrate this point to me. As I sat, I saw a mother Pig feeding her children. It was in the way she laid on the ground and the children (piglets) were sucking that God used the activity to speak to me. I noticed that the Pig just laid down carelessly, opened her legs and closed her eyes and the children went on and on to suck. By the way she laid, I believe a baby goat passing by could have also sucked and she could not have bothered. As I looked at what was going on, I heard the Spirit say to me, "many Christians are poor financially because they think money is free out there in the world for anyone who wants it to go out and get like the Pigs milk. He said wealth is under control and hidden and it is given only to those that qualify to get. It is not through hard work alone that a person becomes rich He said."

I undertook to confirm what the Spirit ministered to me and I found out that it is true. I found that in the world money is given by God or Satan and they give only to their own. For a person to get money from God he will have to be a member of God's family. In the same vein to get money from Satan a person will have to be a member of Satan's family. It is because of this fact that if a person opens his mouth and say he is a Christian then he must live as a true Christian as without doing this he will suffer as he will not be given anything he needs and asks for by either God or Satan. These facts are confirmed by many passages in the Bible.

Some of these are;

(a) Wealth in the world is not open and free, Isaiah 45:3,

" I will give you the treasures of darkness, riches stored in secret places, so that you may know that I am the Lord,

the God of Israel, who summons you by name

(b)Wealth is given by God or Satan,

God gives wealth.

This fact is confirmed by what is said in

Deuteronomy 8:18.

" But remember the Lord your God, for it is he who gives you the ability to produce wealth, and so confirms his covenant, which he swore to your forefathers, as it is today."

Satan gives wealth,

This fact is confirmed by what happened between Jesus and Satan in Matt 4:8-9

" Again, the devil took him to a very high mountain and showed him all the kingdoms of the world and their splendor. "All this I will give you," he said, "if you will bow down and worship me."

(c)God gives to His servants but He gives according to their ability not what the servants wants.

Matthew 25:14-15,

"Again, it (The Kingdom of God) will be like a man going on a journey, who called his servants and entrusted his property to them. To one he gave five talents of money, to another two talents, and to another one talent, each according to his ability. Then he went on his journey."

(d) The world does not want Christians to have money.

If you are a Christian then the first thing you need to know as you set out to look for money is that, Satan who is the prince of this world and is behind the world system, does not want Christians to be rich and as such, Satan and his agents are out to prevent them from making and having money. He does this by making sure that they do not succeed in any business, work or investments or anything they engage in to make money. This means for a Christian to make money, he will have to be in a position whereby Satan and his agents cannot stop him. The only way this can be achieved by a Christian is to make sure that he remains in a healthy relationship with Christ and he does his business, work or investing in partnership with God. This is about doing business, work or investing based on Gods principles. It is only when a person is in Christ that he is able to be successful in all he does.

This fact is confirm in John 15:7 which says,

" If you remain in me and my words remain in you, ask whatever you wish, and it will be given you."

This means if you are a Christian and you will want to make money then you will need to remain in Christ at all times.

(e)Money is value

To make money as a Christian, you will need to know what money really is and how it is made. Money is value and as such the genuine way to make money by a Christian is for him to be able to create and trade value. There are many other ways of making money without the creation of value but they are not godly and should therefore not be adapted by a Christian. Any money made by these other methods bring sorrows to the makers.

(f) Money belongs to God and He gives it for a purpose.

The Bible in Haggai 2:8 says the silver and gold belong to God.

Matthew 25:14 (NIV) makes us to understand that God does not give things, He entrusts.

This means everything a person has is for a purpose as "trusts" are entrusted for a purpose. A Christian who is out to get money must therefore know what God entrust money for. The acquisition of this knowledge will enable him to be a faithful steward thereby fulfilling the requirement needed for him to continue to be a steward and be given more money.

Matthew 25:14-30 and Luke 16:1-2 which I have quoted below confirms these.

(i)Matthew 25:14-30,

"Again, it will be like a man going on a journey, who called his servants and entrusted his property to them. To one he gave five talents of money, to another two talents, and to another one talent, each according to his ability. Then he went on his journey. The man who had received the five talents went at once and put his money to work and gained five more. So also, the one with the two talents gained two more. But the man who had received the one talent went off, dug a hole in the ground and hid his master's money.

"After a long time the master of those servants returned and settled accounts with them. The man who had received the five talents brought the other five. 'Master,' he said, 'you entrusted me with five talents. See, I have gained five more.'

"His master replied, 'Well done, good and faithful servant! You have been faithful with a few things; I will put you in charge of many things. Come and share your master's happiness!'

"The man with the two talents also came. 'Master,' he said, 'you entrusted me with two talents; see, I have gained two more.'

"His master replied, 'Well done, good and faithful servant! You have been faithful with a few things; I will put you in charge of many things. Come and share your master's happiness!'

"Then the man who had received the one talent came. 'Master,' he said, 'I knew that you are a hard man, harvesting where you have not sown and gathering where you have not scattered seed. So I was afraid and went out and hid your talent in the ground. See, here is what belongs to you.'

"His master replied, 'You wicked, lazy servant! So you knew that I harvest where I have not sown and gather where I have not scattered seed? Well then, you should have put my money on deposit with the bankers, so that when I returned I would have received it back with interest.

"'Take the talent from him and give it to the one who has the ten talents. For everyone who has will be given more, and he will have an abundance. Whoever does not have, even what he has will be taken from him."

(ii)Luke 16:1-2,

" Jesus told his disciples: "There was a rich man whose manager was accused of wasting his possessions. So he called him in and asked him, 'What is this I hear about you? Give an account of your management, because you cannot be manager any longer."

These things that I have discussed above make up the first group of things that a Christian that is out to make money must know.

The second group are made up of things a Christian must have to be able to make money.

They are,

Financial literacy.

What is financial literacy? Why is it necessary for making money?

Financial literacy is financial knowledge. The person who has financial knowledge is financially literate.

KNOWLEDGE= INFORMATION+ EDUCATION

This means for a person to be knowledgeable about money he needs to have financial information and education.

The possession of these gives a person financial intelligence which is that part of a person's intelligence which he uses to solve financial problems.

It is different from financial IQ which is the measurement of that intelligence.

There are five basic financial IQs that a person must have to be able to solve his financial problems well.

They are,

(a) knowledge of how to make money

(b) knowledge of how to protect your money

(c) knowledge of how to budget money. This has to do with the allocation and use of money correctly.

(d) knowledge of how to leverage money. Leveraging money has to do with the knowledge and ability to multiply money.

(e) Improving your financial information.

This is about acquiring information about money and remaining well informed always about money.

(iii)The second in the list of the things that a person must have to be able to make money are skills.

There are four skills that a Christian who wants to make money must have.

What these skills are, why they are needed and what they are needed for are discussed and explained below.

(a)self management skills

Self management skills are the skills a person needs to be able to discipline, organize and manage himself to do what he should do when he should do it. Without self management skills a person will not be able to get himself organized to do what he should do correctly when he should do it. The lack of this skill is responsible for why many people are unorganized and unable to discipline and direct themselves to get things done.

(b)Service skills.

Service skills are value creation skills. They are needed for the creation of value. Value is anything that can be used by people for solving a problem or meeting a human need. Service skills are sometimes referred to as problem solving or productivity skills. Their possession by a person enables a person to be able to serve others through which he is able to, solve their problems or produce products that people use to meet needs they have or render services that help people solve problems they have thereby causing money to flow to him. Any person who has a value creation skill and is able to use it to create value which can meet a need or solve a problem for people, he will have money given to him. This person will never lack money as long as he is able to, create this value and find people with the need or problem the value he creates solves or meets and he sells the value to them profitably. He will be able to make money through this or by doing this and he will never lack money because money is value and a reward for service.

To further bring out very clearly the role, relevance, importance and the necessity of possessing service skills by anyone who wants to be able to make money, so that you the reader will understand very clearly the place of service skills in the making of money, I will want to discuss and explain how a person can get money and the ways of making money available to mankind today.

(c) Relationship skills

To make money a person will need to have relationship creation and sustenance skills. These skills enables a person to be able to relate to people and serve them well. Money is with people and as such whoever cannot relate to people well cannot serve them well and if you cannot serve people well you cannot get them to give you money.

(d) Stewardship skills.

Money is a trust from God and as such whoever gets money is expected to use it for what God gives money for. Faithful stewardship of money is using money for what God gives money for. Whoever gets money is expected to steward it faithfully because a day comes when a person who has been entrusted with something will be expected to give account of what has been entrusted to him. How much a person will continue to see of the thing that has been entrusted to him is dependent on how faithful a steward he has been of what has been entrusted to him.

Stewardship skills and faithful stewardship are important when it comes to making money. I will therefore want to use the next chapter to discuss how a person is expected to use the money he gets for him to be a faithful steward. I will explain why God gives money to people and what He expects the money He gives to be used for.

194

195

8:00 HOW YOU A CHRISTIAN SHOULD USE MONEY WHEN YOU MAKE IT

This chapter discusses and explains how a Christian should use the money he makes. If all that we have discussed in this book can be likened to the knowledge a person needs to build a house then what is discussed in this chapter can be likened to the knowledge of how to put up the roof of the house. Having the knowledge to build a house must include the knowledge of how to put up the roof as without this knowledge a person can't say he has the knowledge of how to build a house. This is because a house without a roof is no house, in the same vein knowing how to make money without knowing how to manage or use it correctly is like knowing how to build a house without how to put up the roof.

The knowledge of what has been discussed in this chapter is therefore very important and necessary for achieving financial success by a Christian.

I will therefore advise that you pay attention and try to understand what I will discuss in this chapter because how much money you a Christian will see no matter what you are involved in as your business, work or investments is dependent on how faithful a steward of money you are.

Matthew 25:14 which is quoted below confirms this.

"Again, it will be like a man going on a journey, who called his servants and entrusted his property to them. To one he gave five talents of money, to another two talents, and to another one talent, each according to his ability."

This verse brings out the fact that God entrusts things to people and I hope you know that to entrust is different from giving. When a thing is entrusted it is expected that it should be faithfully stewarded as an account is expected to be given but when it is given it can be used anyhow the receiver wants as the giver relinquishes ownership at the point of giving. From the above verse it is clear that what is entrusted to any servant is dependent on what the servant can manage faithfully and not what he wants. This point is worthy of note by all those reading this book and have been praying to God for money. God will not give you the money you want, He will only give you what you can manage. So let me advice here, if you want to see more money than what you are seeing now then go and improve in your money management ability.

Also when a servant is not able to faithfully steward what is entrusted to him he is sacked, he is deprived of what he is unable to steward faithfully.

Luke 16:1-2 which says,

" Jesus told his disciples: "There was a rich man whose manager was accused of wasting his possessions. So he called him in and asked him, 'What is this I hear about you? Give an account of your management, because you cannot be manager any longer."

A Christian must and should be able to steward money faithfully for him to be entrusted with money. This is because all the money a person makes is not his, he is only a steward and a steward is expected to be faithful,1corinthians 4:1-2,

So then, men ought to regard us as servants of Christ and as those entrusted with the secret things of God. 2 Now it is required that those who have been given a trust must prove faithful.

The question is, what does God entrust money to a person for? Every Christian who wants God to entrust money to him needs to know the answer to this question because faithful stewardship which is about, preserving, improving and using correctly (using for the purpose it has been entrusted) what has been entrusted is key to one being entrusted with anything.

The answer to this question is, God entrusts money to people as a tool and a means to be used for carrying out their assignment in the world. This means when a person gets money he should use a part for enabling him to become the person that he needs to become to do what God has called him to do. For a person to become the person who can live and do what God has called him to do he will have to develop himself. Every human being has been created equipped but not qualified for what he has been created for hence every human being needs personal development to become able to live and fulfill his life purpose. The first use of money should therefore be self development .A part of the money God entrust to a person should be used for developing himself to become qualified to do what he is in the world for.

The second area of focus for use of money God entrust, should be, in helping the person to do what God has created him to do. This will involve the use of money entrusted to a person for the creation and sustenance in a healthy condition all the relationships a person exist in. Man was created and placed in relationships. No person can therefore live and become who he was created to be and do what he was created to do without being in healthy relationships. When entrusted with money a person should therefore use such money in a way that it does not destroy but build and sustain in a healthy condition the relationships that he has been created and placed in.

The third area of focus for the use of the money God entrust to a person is giving. God entrust money to His people so that they can give. Give to who and for what you may be asking.

In Matthew chapter 25 are three parables which Jesus used to teach. All the three parables are about money. They bring out clearly to who and for what a Christian should give money. I will use the remaining part of this chapter to discuss these parables with a view to explaining the things that God expects Christians to use the money He entrust to them for.

(i) Matthew 25:1-13 which I quote below discusses the first parable which is about the ten bridesmaids.

"At that time the kingdom of heaven will be like ten virgins who took their lamps and went out to meet the bridegroom. Five of them were foolish and five were wise. The foolish ones took their lamps but did not take any oil with them. The wise, however, took oil in jars along with their lamps. The bridegroom was a long time in coming, and they all became drowsy and fell asleep.

"At midnight the cry rang out: 'Here's the bridegroom! Come out to meet him!'

"Then all the virgins woke up and trimmed their lamps. The foolish ones said to the wise, 'Give us some of your oil; our lamps are going out.'

"'No,' they replied, 'there may not be enough for both us and you. Instead, go to those who sell oil and buy some for yourselves.'

"But while they were on their way to buy the oil, the bridegroom arrived. The virgins who were ready went in with him to the wedding banquet. And the door was shut.

"Later the others also came. 'Sir! Sir!' they said. 'Open the door for us!'

"But he replied, 'I tell you the truth, I don't know you.'

"Therefore keep watch, because you do not know the day or the hour."

The girls were waiting for the arrival of the groom. Five invested in extra oil while five had the money but they did not. When the groom finally arrived only the five that invested their money in what they were waiting for went in with the groom. Those who did not were locked out.

This parable has a lesson for all Christian as to where and for what they should use their money. Jesus Christ is the groom Christians are waiting for and His gospel which He has asked us to take to the ends of the world is the oil which we should invest in. If we do not, then like the five foolish bridesmaids we will end up outside when Christ comes. The various ways by which we are to give for the gospel and the work of the kingdom of God are enumerated in the Bible. They include Tithes, Offerings and other gifts we can give for needs in the church and the work of the kingdom in general.

(ii)Matthew 25:14-30 which I quote below discusses the second parable,

"Again, it will be like a man going on a journey, who called his servants and entrusted his property to them. To one he gave five talents of money, to another two talents, and to another one talent, each according to his ability. Then he went on his journey. The man who had received the five talents went at once and put his money to work and gained five more. So also, the one with the two talents gained two more. But the man who had received the one talent went off, dug a hole in the ground and hid his master's money.

"After a long time the master of those servants returned and settled accounts with them. The man who had received the five talents brought the other five. 'Master,' he said, 'you entrusted me with five talents. See, I have gained five more.'

"His master replied, 'Well done, good and faithful servant! You have been faithful with a few things; I will put you in charge of many things. Come and share your master's happiness!'

"The man with the two talents also came. 'Master,' he said, 'you entrusted me with two talents; see, I have gained two more.'

"His master replied, 'Well done, good and faithful servant! You have been faithful with a few things; I will put you in charge of many things. Come and share your master's happiness!'

"Then the man who had received the one talent came. 'Master,' he said, 'I knew that you are a hard man, harvesting where you have not sown and gathering where you have not scattered seed. So I was afraid and went out and hid your talent in the ground. See, here is what belongs to you.'

"His master replied, 'You wicked, lazy servant! So you knew that I harvest where I have not sown and gather where I have not scattered seed? Well then, you should have put my money on deposit with the bankers, so that when I returned I would have received it back with interest.

"'Take the talent from him and give it to the one who has the ten talents. For everyone who has will be given more, and he will have an abundance. Whoever does not have, even what he has will be taken from him. And throw that worthless servant outside, into the darkness, where there will be weeping and gnashing of teeth."

This second parable is the parable of the talents. It talks about the second use to which God expects His servants to put the talents(money) He gives them. God expects that part of the money He entrusts to a Christian should be invested so that it can earn more money. It is clear from this parable that God considers investing a very serious and important activity and as such He expects that a part of the money He entrust should be invested.

When this subject of investing is mentioned many say they cannot do it because what they earn is not enough to meet their needs and so they cannot save a part to invest. My advice to you who is reading this book if you are one of such people is, change your lifestyle. It is life style that prevents people from being able to save not the amount being earned. You will need to save and invest because God expects you to. Another reason why you must save and invest is that a time is coming when you can no longer earn as a result of old age or you may no longer have your income due to retirement or your business may no longer be earning you income. You will need to also note that investing is a practice which every Christian should be interested in because investing enables money to work and earn money for the investor. Investing also frees a person from physical involvement in making money thereby having time for other activities. The question that I will want to answer before I bring the discussion in this chapter to a close is, where can a Christian invest? Answering this question is necessary and important because many Christians for not knowing what investing really is, in what and where a Christian can invest and not invest have been victims of scams which are being peddled by what are today referred to as "Wonder Banks." I will not be giving you a list of things or places you can invest , rather I will want to give you guidelines for selecting an investment opportunity that a Christian can invest in.

For a Christian an investment opportunity must meet the following criteria,

(a)There must be a product or service. An investment opportunity that does not have a product or service is not an investment opportunity for Christians.

(b)The product or service of the opportunity must meet a human need or solves a human problem. An investment opportunity that does not have a product or service that meet human need is not an opportunity for a Christian.

(c) The product or service must be able to bring about improvement to people or the environment. Any investment opportunity that has product or service that does not improve human life or the environment is not an investment opportunity for a Christian.

(d) The opportunity should be such that every investor stands to gain. An investment opportunity that does not enable every investor to gain or benefit from his investment is a fraud and as such not an opportunity for a Christian to invest in.

The last advice I will want to give about investing and investment opportunities is, never invest in what you do not understand and never invest an amount you cannot lose.

(iii)Matthew 25:31-46 which I quote below discusses the third and last of the parables which gives Christians guidelines on where and for what they should use the money God entrust to them.

"When the Son of Man comes in his glory, and all the angels with him, he will sit on his throne in heavenly glory. All the nations will be gathered before him, and he will separate the people one from another as a shepherd separates the sheep from the goats. He will put the sheep on his right and the goats on his left.

"Then the King will say to those on his right, 'Come, you who are blessed by my Father; take your inheritance, the kingdom prepared for you since the creation of the world. For I was hungry and you gave me something to eat, I was thirsty and you gave me something to drink, I was a stranger and you invited me in, I needed clothes and you clothed me, I was sick and you looked after me, I was in prison and you came to visit me.'

"Then the righteous will answer him, 'Lord, when did we see you hungry and feed you, or thirsty and give you something to drink? When did we see you a stranger and invite you in, or needing clothes and clothe you? When did we see you sick or in prison and go to visit you?'

"The King will reply, 'I tell you the truth, whatever you did for one of the least of these brothers of mine, you did for me.'

"Then he will say to those on his left, 'Depart from me, you who are cursed, into the eternal fire prepared for the devil and his angels. For I was hungry and you gave me nothing to eat, I was thirsty and you gave me nothing to drink, I was a stranger and you did not invite me in, I needed clothes and you did not clothe me, I was sick and in prison and you did not look after me.'

"They also will answer, 'Lord, when did we see you hungry or thirsty or a stranger or needing clothes or sick or in prison, and did not help you?'

"He will reply, 'I tell you the truth, whatever you did not do for one of the least of these, you did not do for me.'

"Then they will go away to eternal punishment, but the righteous to eternal life."

This parable is the parable of sheep and goats. Jesus used it to illustrate what is going to happen when He returns to the Earth for the final judgment. He said the goats will be sent to eternal punishment and their crime is that, He was hungry and they did not give him what to eat, he was thirsty and they gave him nothing to drink, he was a stranger and they did not invite him in ,He needed clothes and they did not clothe him, He was sick and in prison and they did not look after him.

If you look carefully at all the things that the goats did not do that resulted in them being sent to eternal punishment, you will see that they are things that a person needs money to do them. So these people who are being referred to as goats were not able to do them because they either had no money or they had money but did not use it for the things that they should use their money for just as the five foolish bridesmaids.

This parable is saying that part of the money God entrust to you should be used to meet the needs of the needy.

The question is, who are the needy ?

The needy that a Christian must take a part of the money entrusted to him to provide for their needs include the following,

Members of his family.

Those who have needs at a given time and God brings them to his attention.

These are the category of the needy who a Christian should provide for. A needy person is not just anybody who ask you for money, a needy person is one with a need that God brings your way and directs that you give of the money He has entrusted to you to meet the need. You will need to heed this advice because Satan knows that giving is a requirement for becoming a faithful steward so he sends people I call devourers after Christians who are ignorant of how to give and who to give and gets them to give to wrong people and purposes thereby making them to be unfaithful servants as giving wrongly amounts to wasting of God's money. Giving is right only when it is done for the right reason for the right purpose.

These are the ways that God expects those that are entrusted with money to use the money entrusted to them.

The last two chapters are focused at the things that a person must do to achieve financial success. The question is, what will enable a person to be able to do these things? There are many people who know what to do but they never get to do them. Knowing is not enough to do. I will therefore want to use the remaining part of this chapter to discuss the things that a person needs to be able to do the things that he needs to do to achieve financial success. I will also discuss how a person can acquire them.

For a person to carry out any activity successfully he needs capacity, commitment, competence, tools and resources. In the same vein for a person to be able to make and manage money successfully, he needs, the commitment, capacity, competence, resources and tools to make and manage money faithfully (God's way).

For commitment the person needs a reason for why he needs to make and manage money God's way. When a person knows what life is, how it should be lived and why it should be lived correctly, he will have the commitment to live and do the things that will enable him make and manage money faithfully. There are three ways that people use money , they can waste it, this is when they use the money they make to buy liabilities and things that are perishables. They can spend it, this is when they use their money to only pay bills and other necessities or they can invest it, this is when they use it for the purpose money is entrusted to man. Capacity enables a person to be able to discipline himself and invest it, that it do the right things with money rather than waste or just spend it. With the ability to discipline self a person is able to make right choices when it comes to the use of the money he makes. For capacity he needs character and heart of those who live and do things God's way. A person will be able to acquire these when he becomes a citizen of God's kingdom by being born again and then renews his mind and lives a Godly or holy life. For competence he needs the skills for self and relationship management and service. Skills are a product of training and experience and as such for competence in making and managing money God's way a person who is a citizen of God's kingdom will need training and practice. The resource that a person who has commitment, capacity and competence needs to be able to make and manage money correctly and successfully is, financial literacy (knowledge about money) while the tools he needs are a financial plan and a budget.

229

9:00 HOW YOU A CHRISTIAN SHOULD LIVE AND LOOK FOR MONEY.

Money is a means and a necessity that shows up as a needed resource for everything that man would ever want to do while in this world.

Ecclesiastes 10:19 which I quote below confirms this

"A feast is made for laughter,

and wine makes life merry,

but money is the answer for everything."

Money is therefore a necessity which every human being living on earth, Christians inclusive must have.

The problem however is that no human being was born with money and as such all humans will have to look for it while they are here on earth.

Experience has however revealed that looking for money can be a dangerous activity if not understood and done correctly.

If not understood and done correctly looking for money can occupy all of a person's time thereby making him to not only be a slave to money but unable to do any other thing well.

From what we read in the Bible and experience, life and living for a human being should not all be about looking for money, a human being has other things which he needs to also do in life to have a fulfilled and meaningful life and as such he cannot and should not spend all his time looking for money which is not only temporal but cannot be used to acquire all the things that man needs for a satisfactory, meaningful and fulfilling life.

A Christian should therefore not spend all his time each day going after money and the things money can be used to do or acquire. Life and living is more than things and it should therefore not just be about the accumulation of things.

Luke 12:23-31, which I quote below confirms this,

Life is more than food, and the body more than clothes. Consider the ravens: They do not sow or reap, they have no storeroom or barn; yet God feeds them. And how much more valuable you are than birds! Who of you by worrying can add a single hour to his life? Since you cannot do this very little thing, why do you worry about the rest?

Consider how the lilies grow. They do not labor or spin. Yet I tell you, not even Solomon in all his splendor was dressed like one of these. If that is how God clothes the grass of the field, which is here today, and tomorrow is thrown into the fire, how much more will he clothe you, O you of little faith! And do not set your heart on what you will eat or drink; do not worry about it. For the pagan world runs after all such things, and your Father knows that you need them. But seek his kingdom, and these things will be given to you as well.

For a Christian to be able to live life correctly, he should plan his life so that he is able to plan the use of his time such that he is able to look for money and also make time for the other things he needs to do to live and fulfill his life purpose.

Life has a purpose and the fulfillment of this purpose should be every Christian's priority as he lives. Many who spend all their time chasing and worrying about money have not only ended up not seeing money but they have ended up with lives that are full of problems. This has happened because they have had all their attention and time taken by looking for money and have neglected other areas of their lives that they need to also give attention to.

Jesus in **Mathew 4:4 says, "It is written: 'Man does not live on bread alone'.**

This means a Christian should not live and use all his time for looking for bread (physical things, money inclusive).

For a Christian to be able to live and do all that he needs to do to live life correctly he should plan his life and have a life plan which should be his strategy or guide in living life. This plan should be his guide in all that he does, even in the use of his time on a daily basis.

Life planning enables a person to structure his life and control how and what he uses his time for even on a daily basis. It enables a person to have a strategy by which to live by to be able to do well all the things that he should do to not only make money which he needs to acquire the things that he needs for his physical sustenance but also get all the other things he needs to meet his other needs which are not physical.

Living by this strategy will also enable him to become the person that he needs to become to be able to live and fulfill his life purpose.

For details of what life planning really is and how you can define and plan your life, you may wish to attend the authors workshop titled, "WIN@LIFE WIN@WORK"

The Bible in Matthew 6:33 which I quote below, gives us a guide on how we should live and what we should live for to get money and all the other things we need for life.

"But seek first His kingdom and his righteousness, and all these things will be given to you as well."

I will want to conclude our discussion on how you a Christian should live and look for money by saying, you need to plan and structure your life such that you are able to live a balanced life. A balanced life is one that is being lived in such a way that adequate time is made for all its dimensions. For you to be able to do this you will need a strategy. A life strategy is called a life plan, it enables a person to discipline and organize himself ,prioritize his time and activities to be able to use his time in a balanced way.

Failure to do this will result in a person not being able to live and take care of all areas of his life adequately.

Let this serve as a word of counsel and at the same time a

warning to you a Christian that will want to look for money as many who have not heeded this advice for balance and prioritization in the way that they should live and look for money have ended up spending almost all their time looking for money and their lives are focused and centered only on looking for money. The activities they do for money have become the center of their lives rather than these being only an aspect. They have because of this had their lives ruined .

I would therefore want to close this chapter with a word of advice to you about looking for money, LIVE YOUR LIFE IN A BALANCED WAY AS YOU LOOK FOR MONEY. Your

business or work which you do for
money should be an aspect of
your life not the main focus of
your life.

241

10:00 CASE STUDY

The Bible presents us with a very good case which I will want to use as a case study for explaining the requirements for making money. The case contains all the requirements a Christian must have to be able to live and make money.

The case also brings out what the Church should help Christians to have in place for them to be able to live and make money. I will want to use this last chapter of this book to discuss and analyze this case for all those who will read this book to not only know but understand the requirements for making and managing money by a Christian.

The case is found in 2kings 4:1-7 and is quoted below,

" The wife of a man from the company of the prophets cried out to Elisha, "Your servant my husband is dead, and you know that he revered the Lord. But now his creditor is coming to take my two boys as his slaves."

Elisha replied to her, "How can I help you? Tell me, what do you have in your house?"

"Your servant has nothing there at all," she said, "except a little oil."

Elisha said, "Go around and ask all your neighbors for empty jars. Don't ask for just a few. Then go inside and shut the door behind you and your sons. Pour oil into all the jars, and as each is filled, put it to one side."

She left him and afterward shut the door behind her and her sons. They brought the jars to her and she kept pouring. When all the jars were full, she said to her son, "Bring me another one."

But he replied, "There is not a jar left." Then the oil stopped flowing.

She went and told the man of God, and he said, "Go, sell the oil and pay your debts. You and your sons can live on what is left."

EXPLANATION AND ANALYSIS OF THE CASE

I will want to go through this story verse by verse to bring out the requirements that a Christian must have, the things that such a Christian must be able to do and the steps such a Christian needs to follow to be able to make and manage money faithfully.

I will also explain the attributes such a Christian must have and how a Christian should use them to be able to live, make and manage money correctly(faithfully).

VERSE ONE:

THIS VERSE PRESENTS THE SITUATION IN THE STORY AS,

A CASE OF UNPAID DEBT WHICH A WOMAN FOUND HERSELF IN. SHE NEEDED TO PAY THE DEBT OR ELSE HER CHILDREN WILL BE TAKEN INTO SLAVERY . SHE SOUGHT HELP FROM THE PROPHET ELISHA.THE VERSE ALSO TELLS US WHO THIS WOMAN AND HER FAMILY ARE.

The story in verse one brings out very clearly the case,

" A widow whose husband, a man who loved the Lord, but poor and had borrowed a large sum of money had died and left her with the debt". The man had died, maybe from the stress of being unable to get what he needs to meet his family needs which resulted in him going into borrowing. The debt no doubt was large as the debtor threatened to take the man's children (two boys) to become his slaves.

The woman had no means of earning income (no business, no work).

This is a clear case of need, which can lead a person into financial bondage and the bondage of poverty and if care is not taken, the person can hand it over to his family at death just as this man who had died did, thereby promoting the cycle of poverty in the family.

Many people in our society are in this condition. Who knows, maybe you who is reading this book is in this condition or you know someone who is in this position. If you are or you know someone who is, then don't worry for after you finish reading this book you will know what to do to solve the problem for yourself and the other people you know.

The verse also tells us that,

THE FAMILY LOVES THE LORD.

The question you may be asking here is why should a person who loves the Lord be poor? This man and his family ended up poor and had to borrow money to live on even though he loved the Lord because you need more than loving the Lord to be entrusted with resources in the kingdom of God.

There are requirements that a person who is a citizen of the kingdom of God must have to qualify for resources in the Kingdom of God. These requirements are made up of things such a person must know and be able to do to have resources entrusted to him once he becomes a citizen of the kingdom of God.

A look at the story reveals these requirements that a person must have and be able to do to make money. I will want to use the last part of this book to analyze the story for you to have a clear understanding of these requirements and the roles they play in enabling a citizen of Gods kingdom to be entrusted with resources.

HOW THE WOMAN SET OUT TO SOLVE THE MONEY PROBLEM SHE HAS.

Determined to solve her problem, the woman ran to the Prophet for help. I believe this woman went to the prophet not one of her relatives or a rich person in her community because she knows no man can provide her with a permanent solution to her money problem. Man can provide her with an answer to the effects of her problem but not a solution to the problem. The solution to a problem deals with the cause of the problem while an answer addresses the effects of the problem.

The question is why did this woman choose to go to the prophet? I believe she did because,

She has a relationship with God and she trusts God. Verse one of the story makes us to know that her family loves the Lord.

She knows that God's method for solving a problem is the best approach.

NOTE:

This verse brings out the fact that access to money when a person has become a citizen of Gods kingdom is to have a personal relationship with God.

Approaches created by the world for making money can enable a person to make money and in most cases without using God's principles. The problem with these approaches if they are used by a citizen of Gods kingdom is that monies made this way always end up bringing to their possessors problems as they are not blessings from God.

Proverbs 10:22(NKJV) which is quoted below brings this out clearly,

" The blessing of the Lord makes one rich,

And He adds no sorrow with it."

VERSE TWO

This verse brings out the fact that what a person needs to solve a problem he has, money problems inclusive , is already with him. It is in something God has already placed it in his hands but it will take,

God to reveal to him what it is and its potential.

Renewed mindset for him to value what God reveals to him and use it as a means for solving his money problem. This is important and a very necessary requirement for making money. This is because most people do not value the things they have including themselves. When a person does not value himself or what he has, he will not be able to give himself the inner consent he needs to succeed in what he embarks upon and even in life as a whole. He will not also be able to either see the potential in what he has or use it profitably.

The prophet by the question he asked in verse two, "What do you have in your house?" is out to get the woman to take a look at what she has and to also find out if she is one of those who values and sees potential in what they have to solve their problems . He wanted to ascertain this fact about the knowledge and value of resources with the widow before he asked her to do anything. This approach is far removed from the approach we use today, where when a person comes to us with a problem or a need, say for money, we just give them money or give them what to do to get money. This approach will not help them as we have succeeded in meeting their immediate need but we leave them with the cause of their problem. They will go and continue living the way they had lived which led to them having the problem of the lack of money which they came to us with. We need to change them and show them what to do rather than just giving them the money they need. This approach is necessary, because the lack of money is caused by who a person is, which is revealed by his mindset and how he lives and does things before what the person does to make money.

NOTE:

This verse brings out a principle and a fact which we must bring to the knowledge of all those we want to empower and help to make money.

The principle / fact is

God will use what you already have to enable you earn and make money. So if you desire to make money ask God for the revelation of what you already have which with God's blessing you can use to make money.

To make money you must see yourself a person who can make money. You must see yourself worthy of having money. If you do not see yourself worthy, you will and can never make money and become wealthy no matter what you find to do.

VERSE THREE:

This verse brings out two requirements which all those who want to know how to make money must have.

It is, good and healthy relationships.

The assignment the prophet gave the woman to go and borrow empty containers from her neighbors, is to confirm whether the relationships in her life are healthy. If the woman had not been living with her neighbors well she wouldn't have been able to go and borrow empty containers from them.

Good relationships are necessary and vital to all human beings as they live on earth. It is through people that God provides you with all your needs, money inclusive. It is through people that God trains you to become a better person (develop and acquire Godly character traits). It is also through people who you serve that you fulfill your purpose on earth and bring glory to God, hence the need and ability to create and sustain good relationships with others is important for anyone who wants to be able to make money .All the money you need and you will ever need is with people who are your neighbors not God. Having good relationships with your neighbors can enable you to access them and their money when you call on them with the solutions to their problems which you have and call business.

The second thing that this verse has brought out as a requirement for anyone who wants to be able to make money is,

WILLINGNESS TO ACT on God's INSTRUCTIONS, OBEDIENCE TO GOD. YOU MUST OBEY WHAT EVER GOD TELLS YOU TO DO WHETHER IT MAKES SENSE TO YOU OR NOT TO PROSPER IN LIFE.

For any person to be able to make money he must be willing to act on what the Word of God tells him to do, whether it makes sense to him or not. The prophet gave the woman a task which required her putting forward or displaying these two requirements. It must be noted that God does not give people what they ask Him for directly, He gives them directives or instructions which when obeyed results in them getting what they asked for. Obedience and being able to obey is therefore a key ability and step on the way to making and managing money.

VERSES FOUR AND FIVE:

These verses bring out what people who want to help people

become people who can make money must and should do for them. In verse four the prophet directed the woman to go and work. He gave her a business and tells her how to do it. She is to work on the business with her children and behind closed doors not open to everyone. This brings out the requirement that, you must be an effective participant in the economy where money circulates to have access to money. The possession of a business or work enables a person to be an effective participant in the economy. Working together with children develops family ties and help pass on the legacy of work. The woman in verse five again displayed the vital requirement of

OBEDIENCE. Working with her children is about her empowering her children to also become effective participants in the economy and thereby become people who can make money. This is the best thing anyone with children should seek to do to them rather than leaving them lots of money as inheritance. Teach your children how to work and make money thereby enabling them to become people who can make money.

These verses also bring out the fact that we should at all times look for ways to help people to be empowered to use their talents and what they have profitably when they come to us with needs especially money rather than giving them handouts. This is because when people get empowered to use their talents and resources they end up becoming able to make money, have sources of wealth and become active and effective participants in the economy. This leads to them becoming financially successful people rather than them just having financial success . A person who only has the representation of money (the decorated paper) but not the ability to make money (create value) only has financial success while those who have the ability to create value and the representation of money (decorated paper) have become financially successful people.

Enabling people to become effective participants in the economy is called true economic empowerment and it is the correct approach to enabling people to overcome poverty.

VERSE SIX:

This verse brings out a requirement for becoming a financially successful person and indeed a person who can succeed in life. It is a requirement which people who want to become true money makers and be able to make money and have financial success must note.

You must have a vision for your life. This will enable you to have a better picture of your life situation than what you are in presently. It will serve as a destination for you in life. Failure to have this will not only limit you but even God in your life.

Do not limit yourself and God by how you think and perceive about life. By thinking small, seeing small and planning for small you end up limiting God. God will not give you what you do not have the capacity for and your capacity is revealed by your vision, what you can see. This fact is brought out clearly in this verse by the fact that the oil ceased when all the containers she collected finished. If she had borrowed more containers, the oil could have continued to flow! Many people have limited the blessings and in particular the money God can allow into their lives by seeing, thinking, and planning small. For a person to become a financially successful person he must learn to have big dreams and think big even if what he has or is doing is small and he can only act small for a start.

VERSE SEVEN:

This verse carries the prophet's last instruction to the woman. It brings out a vital requirement that those who want to become financially successful must have. It is SKILL! The prophet's instruction brought out the fact that if the woman is to become able to get money then she must have

Commercial Skills – these are skills of buying and selling. A person needs these skills to be involved in commerce and at a profitable level. Without being in commerce (able to buy and sell) a person can't earn money.

Stewardship Skills – these are skills for managing faithfully what a person earns using his commercial skills profitably to sustain the flow of money into his life.

A person is expected to steward what he earns well as doing this allows him to sustain the flow of money into his life. Faithful stewardship of the money he earns will require that he,

(a) Uses a part for the things he must do, these are the debts he must pay. These include, providing for his family's daily needs, giving to the needy, give to God His portion (tithes, offerings).

(b) Uses a part for investing. This is to multiply a part of what he had earned using his commercial skills so that he will have a source of income even when he can no longer work (these were discussed in the chapter on how to manage money).

This story presents to us all that a person must know, have, be and do to be able to live, make and manage money correctly.

As we come to the end of this book and the end of our

discussion about, money, what it is, whose is it, why you must be bothered about it, how to get it and how to use or manage it correctly, I will want to pray for you that has read this book to the end.

My prayer for you is that you put into practice all that you have learned from reading this book for it is only by doing this that you will be able to make and manage money correctly and become a financially successful person who is able to escape the problems money can bring to a person's life.

www.ingramcontent.com/pod-product-compliance
Lightning Source LLC
Chambersburg PA
CBHW051633170526
45167CB00001B/178